The Vernor's Story

The

VE

RNOR'S

Story

from

gnomes

to now

Lawrence L. Rouch

The University of Michigan Press   Ann Arbor

Library of Congress Cataloguing-in-Publication Data

Rouch, Lawrence L.
     The Vernor's story : from gnomes to now / Lawrence L. Rouch
          p.   cm.
     Includes bibliographical references.
     ISBN 0-472-06697-8 (pbk. : acid-free paper)
     1. Vernor's (Firm)—History.   2. Soft drink industry—United States—History   I. Title

HD9349.S634V477   2004
338.4'766362'0973—dc22   2003053358

Designed by Felice E. Lau

     ISBN 978-0-472-06697-1 (pbk. : acid-free paper)

To Bev

Contents

From
Wooden Kegs
to Soda Fountains

The Beginning
of Vernor's

Founding Father
of Detroit's Drink

James Vernor I

Ask someone who grew up in Michigan about childhood memories of favorite foods, and before too long you'll hear about Vernor's Ginger Ale. You'll hear about the ultra-fizzy bubbles in the drink that made unsuspecting children sneeze, about frothy Boston coolers made with Vernor's and vanilla ice cream, hot mugs of Vernor's on icy winter nights, and small glasses of Vernor's dispensed by loving parents to soothe upset tummies. The smells and tastes and sights of childhood remain some of our most intense memories, and the pale gold, gingery fizz of Vernor's Ginger Ale and the jolly gnome who served as corporate mascot remain fond recollections for many who call Michigan their home state. The gnome has since disappeared from the scene, but today's green and gold bottles and cans, proudly labeled "Barrel Aged, Bold Taste" and "The Original Ginger Soda," celebrate a pioneering product that survives even in today's tough soft-drink market. This ultra-fizzy, gingery-tart soda pop is the oldest soft drink in the U.S., with devoted fans across the nation who search grocery store shelves and beseech visiting relatives from Michigan for a stash of their beloved "real" ginger ale. In fact, a popular Internet quiz states that one sure sign of someone from Michigan is placing an order for ginger ale and expecting Vernor's to be served. The story of Vernor's and its corporate growth in Detroit is a part of Michigan history, dating back to the days just after the Civil War when a pharmacist named James Vernor invented his unique ginger soda that came to be known as Detroit's Drink.

James Vernor was born on April 11, 1843, in Albany, New York. His father, a bookkeeper, was descended from a monied family

Detroit artist William Moss painted the Bob-Lo ferry *Ste. Claire* docked at the foot of Woodward with the Vernor's factory in the background. The electric "Vernor's" sign was a well-known landmark until the destruction of the building in the 1950s.

Detroit's Traditions, by William Moss, courtesy of Martha Polacsek of Captain of the Fleet, Inc.

from northern England and Ireland, the Vernors (or Werners), who had arrived from Germany with William of Orange in the 1500s. Early in the 1700s brothers John and Samuel immigrated to Albany, where John operated an inn. He and his wife, Martha, had seven children, the oldest christened John, following a family tradition of naming one son John. A grandson of John and Martha fathered James, who became the founder of the Vernor's Ginger Ale Company.

When James was five his family moved to Detroit, which in 1848 was a town of about 55,000 growing on the riverbanks.

Little is known of James's early childhood other than that he attended the Old Capitol School (named for its quarters, the original Michigan State Capitol Building), where one of his first paid jobs was lighting the schoolhouse stoves at daybreak. This earned him a small salary and prefigured his lifelong work ethic. As a teenager, James ran errands for the Higby and Stearn's Drug Store, later the Frederick Stearn Company. With his zeal for packaging and delivering, he soon advanced to junior clerk, a lofty position for a boy his age, and eventually received training at the drugstore in chemistry and pharmacy. The Vernor's Ginger Ale formula may have occurred to him as he worked with potions in the drugstore basement.[1]

Two legends have been passed down about the origin of Vernor's Ginger Ale. In the first, James Vernor is said to have developed the first batch while working at Higby and Stearn's, storing it in a small oak keg where it brewed while he served in the Union Army. Returning four years later, he discovered his drink had matured to that "deliciously different" flavor. In the other version, Vernor carried the idea in his head throughout the war and first brewed the formula after returning to Detroit and establishing his own drugstore.

I'm originally from Detroit. Whenever I was sick and home from school, Dr. Allison used to come over and give me a shot, telling me that he would be back the next day if I hadn't cured myself by then. (Remember house visits?) To prove that he wasn't totally evil, he would tell my mother that I could have all the Vernor's I wanted. . . .
—Frank W. Donovan

The first legend is more exciting and nicely fits the "Aged 4 Years in Wood" claim that the company promoted since its beginning, but the second is more plausible. James would probably not have

The young James Vernor in his Civil War Union
Army uniform before going off to the war
Courtesy of the Detroit Public Library

left his experimental keg of soda in an employer's basement while
going to war. James's son said in 1936, "I suspect that all through
the war he carried in his mind that formula for the soft drink,"
implying the formula had not yet been mixed while Vernor was at
war.[2] A 1962 interview with James Vernor Davis, president of

the company from 1952 to 1966, also dismisses this theory.[3] The one certain part of the story is the aging in oak barrels over four years. Somehow, Vernor discovered that this developed the flavors he wanted, and the company still uses this method today.

Whether he developed his successful beverage before the Civil War or after, Vernor's strong work ethic may have led him to enlist in 1862, or perhaps he joined the Union Army out of a sense of duty and adventure.[4] He enlisted in the Fourth Michigan Cavalry, which assigned him as a hospital steward because of his drugstore experience.

On New Year's Day, 1863, after having served the last year or so in the Union Army hospital units, James was captured during a battle at LaVergne, Tennessee, by Wheeler and Wharton's Cavalry. Released within a few days and captured again on January 5, he managed to escape this time and make his way into Murfreesboro, near a Confederate POW camp and the site of fierce fighting. The Union Army finally took this city from the Confederate Army, and Vernor emerged from the attic where he had hidden for three days.

Vernor often credited the war with strengthening his discipline and drive. The army was quick to recognize his merits, promoting him to second lieutenant and giving him command of his unit, Brigade Company M, in 1864. In the final year of the Civil War, the Fourth Michigan Cavalry found its place in history by capturing Confederate president Jefferson Davis and his family on May 10, 1865. When James Vernor was mustered out of the Union Army in July of 1865 he returned to Detroit, where he used his discipline and drive in developing "Detroit's Drink."

The soft-drink industry originated in Europe at least as early as the sixteenth century with the popularity of mineral water as a healthful and curative drink. The discovery of its natural fizz led to the hunt for an artificial method of introducing fizz into water as early as the middle 1600s. The most common production method of this period was treating chalk with sulfuric acid and capturing the gaseous product. This gas had not yet been identified as carbon dioxide and was given distinctive names by different manufacturers. Consumers drank the popular bubbly waters to cure everything from dyspepsia to gout.

Mr. Bewley's Julep, developed about 1767 by Richard Bewley of Norfolk, England, was probably the first commercial soda. Many natural mineral waters contained undesirable impurities, which helped the popularity of manufactured ones. Most of the early formulas contained various salts, mainly soda, potash, lithium, or barium salts, which led to the terms *soda* and *soda water*

My dad used to give me Vernor's when I was sick, but I didn't like it because it was too fizzy. So he solved that by using two half-full glasses and pouring the Vernor's back and forth to defizz it for me until I would drink it.
—Corinne Kiefer

The pharmacy at 235 Woodward Avenue
Courtesy of the Detroit Public Library

for these beverages. Storage problems and lack of convenient carbonation methods were the main obstacles to these early efforts.
Only around 1782 did Lavoisier identify the fizz or "fixed air" in
mineral water as carbon dioxide. The addition early in the 1800s
of syrups and flavorings to these popular tonics gave them a new
popularity as refreshments.

Manchester apothecary Thomas Henry founded the first commercial carbonated water manufacturing operation in 1764, but
Jacob Schweppe, a German watchmaker and amateur scientist,
developed the first commercially viable method around 1783.[5]
His bottled beverage was a success, and when Victoria became
queen in 1837 she granted Schweppes & Co. the Royal Warrant
of Appointment (still valid) as purveyors of Her Majesty's soda
water.[6] Schweppes and others faced challenges in bottling that

would not be met until machine-age refinements of bottle-
capping, but when successfully stoppered, these mass-produced
drinks opened with a distinctive pop-
ping sound. This familiar sound
led to the slang terms of *pop*
and *soda pop*.

*I still drink Vernor's Ginger Ale
when da tummy don't feel too good.
It helps. —Ken (from "da UP")*

Interest in mineral water
spread to the colonies,
where suppliers tapped springs
to meet the growing demand. A
source of water at Saratoga, New York, believed by
the Mohawk Indians to have healing powers was "discovered"
by the immigrants from Europe, and many entrepreneurs sold it
under different labels. Another well-known source was Poland
Springs in Maine; its waters, like Saratoga's, are still available in
stores today.

By Vernor's time, novel beverages were proliferating as his fel-
low pharamacists and others throughout the country concocted
thousands of new tonics, some wholesome, some both harm-
less and worthless, and some toxic. Promising to cure anything
from baldness to dementia, these tonics might contain anything
from opiates to arsenic, even uranium. Alcohol appeared in many
formulas, enough to preserve the beverage and often enough
to inebriate the consumer. Atlanta tonic purveyor John Styth
Pemberton added cocaine (then a common ingredient in patent
medicines) to his formula. Pemberton served in the Civil War
near where James Vernor's group captured Jefferson Davis. His
concoction, Coca-Cola, would fare better than his Confederate
cause.

The antebellum bottling industry in the U.S. comprised about
150 companies. By the early 1880s there were over five hundred,

by 1890 at least 1,400, and by 1900 almost three thousand. In 1900 these companies bottled $25 million worth of nonalcoholic beverages a year compared with about $800,000 in the mid-1800s. James Vernor entered the industry just as it began to take off, finding his new career after his service in the Civil War.

Upon returning to Detroit, Vernor quickly resumed work in the pharmacy business, opening a drugstore on the corner of Woodward Avenue and Clifford Street with Charles L'Hommedieu.[7] They bought their own carbonation equipment and began dispensing their own soft drinks. Whether Vernor had retrieved his legendary wooden keg at the end of the war or actually began formulating his ginger ale at this point, this was the beginning of the Vernor's empire.

It's strange, but the two foods indigenous to Michigan which I enjoy most are both quite dangerous. Vernor's ginger soda is infused with a powerful form of carbonation that causes painful paroxysms of coughing if inhaled. The other, rhubarb, is a delicious vegetable which also happens to be quite poisonous if the wrong part is eaten. The fact that some of my fondest childhood memories are established around these hazardous comestibles probably explains a great deal about the person I've grown up to be.
—J. Parish

Ginger ale had its origins in ginger beer, which appeared as early as 1790, when it was first produced by a brewer named William Pitt in England. Two beverage firms in the home of Vernor's ancestors, Grattan (of Belfast) and Cantrell and Cochrane (of Belfast and Dublin), developed ginger ale around 1852. Who developed the formula first is in dispute, but both companies may have developed their drinks to take advantage of mechanical carbonation. Ginger beer relied on natural carbonation, and its cloudiness made it less appetizing to look at than ginger ale. As the so-called Dublin and Belfast ginger ales became the favored drink of the era, many Irish and British firms began

The original Vernor's Pharmacy. This drawing
appeared in many promotional materials.

to export them to thirsty Americans. By the late 1800s ginger ale
imports to the U.S. amounted to over 300,000 bottles per year,
worth nearly half a million dollars.

Early soda expert Charles Herman Sulz relates that ginger ale
formulas generally contained extract of ginger, ginger oil essence,

James Vernor II
Courtesy of the Detroit Public Library

and lemon and rose essences with traces of tincture of capsicum (the fiery pepper-derivative that also gives many personal defense sprays their punch) often added for additional pungency.[8] Other makers added different spices and fruit flavorings. The Belfast-style ginger ales contained ginger root, nutmeg, cinnamon, orange peel, and vanilla among other ingredients.

The exact formula for Vernor's Ginger Ale is a mystery to those outside the company. One writer claims it is a "mixture of nineteen ingredients, including two kinds of ginger root, a type of cayenne pepper, and vanilla," with the ginger and pepper extract percolated through grain for ten days and then placed in oak barrels to age over four years before the final mixing and bottling.[9] An early formula for the final mix published in a newsletter celebrating the company's centennial called for four ounces of aged extract, eight pounds of sugar, an ounce of citric acid, and nine gallons of water.[10] A formula in the *Standard Manual of Soda and Other Beverages* by Dr. Emil Hiss in 1897 calls for nine pounds of granulated sugar, four ounces of a solution of citric acid, and ten gallons of water.[11] Further directions state that the fountain operator was to dissolve the mixture in cold water, strain it through a cloth into the fountain, and charge it with carbonic acid gas to 120 pounds.

An ad from when the pharmacy had become more of a general store

James Vernor was the first licensed pharmacist in Michigan, and he held to precise scientific standards in the pro-duction of his ginger ale. Vernor insisted on only the finest ingredients, in exactly the specified amounts, to ensure consistent good flavor.

The uniform quality and unique blend of flavorings and spices proved popular with consumers, who noticed the strong ginger snap most of all. The formula also included a touch of vanilla, which added a slightly sweet flavor without being overwhelming. The capsicum and the forceful fizz were responsible for Vernor's well-known ability to cause sneezing or even a case of the hiccups, but that didn't stop the new beverage from growing rapidly in popularity.

The Woodward Avenue location was a smart choice, and Detroit had grown up around it by 1870. Vernor soon bought out his partner, and by 1873 his business was solid. He married Emily Walker Smith that same year, and in 1877 James Vernor II was born, followed in 1880 by Emily Louise Vernor. Within a few decades the son would build the business into a huge success.

By 1895 the drugstore had become more of a general store, and Vernor's Ginger Ale had become a household name in Detroit as distribution reached many local outlets. Almost every pharmacy had a soda fountain from the 1890s to the late 1950s. The allure of Vernor's drink had become legendary in the city, and sales were growing rapidly.

The successful pharmacist discouraged his son and namesake from studying to become a pharmacist. When he was still a teen-ager, James Vernor II entered his father's business, and in 1896 they closed the drugstore to pursue the soft-drink industry full time. A small ginger ale brewery was established a few doors from the original pharmacy, and Vernor and his nineteen-year-old son began the full-time manufacturing of Vernor's Ginger Ale. At first the business had just three workers: the two Vernors and a horse named Dick who pulled the delivery wagon. All three worked long hours to meet the growing demand for their deli-ciously different drink.

The Vernors faced local competition from Cronk and Kirtz, makers of sarsaparilla-flavored Dr. Kronk's. To the south, in Dayton, Ohio, a firm called Sachs, Pruden, and Company was bot-tling America's Favorite Ginger Ale. The Vernors and their ginger ale prevailed; neither competitor's product is available today.

The closing of his pharmacy and the success of the ginger ale business also provided the opportunity for James Vernor Sr. to pursue his continuing interest in city politics and a long second-ary career of public service. His local fame due to his popular beverage was nearly surpassed by his reputation as a controver-sial politician and public servant. Vernor's interest in city affairs may initially have been a response to the frequent flooding of the basements of his and neighboring businesses as a result of inadequate city sewer systems. Not getting any satisfaction from the alderman in his district, Vernor ran successfully for alderman himself in 1888. A member of the Michigan Republican Party, he served as a Ward Two alderman and as a member of the Detroit Common Council for twenty-five of the next thirty-five years until his resignation in January 1924, attending to business and other interests during his years off.[12] It was not long after his first victory before the sewer service improved.

Remember going down to the Woodward plant on a hot summer night and getting a Boston cooler: ice cream and Vernor's? Yum, yum.
—Sonya Grieves

Vernor's political career included many confrontations with Detroit mayors and members of the city council, as well as notable achievements for Detroit and contributions to the city. He advocated for and then helped create the city railway system that replaced horse-drawn carriages. Vernor urged private ownership of the transportation system, believing that public ownership would breed corruption and inefficiency. Mayor Pingree disagreed, and a great deal of animosity developed between the two. When the issue came to a vote, only Vernor opposed the mayor; this eventually cost Vernor his elected position. After that Vernor and Pingree spoke little to each other beyond what was necessary for city business. This battle became well known to the electorate, and Vernor was voted out of office mainly for opposing city-owned transportation. Despite this setback Vernor reentered public office as an elected member of the common council in 1904.

He is also credited with building a modern water filtration

system in Detroit, applying his soft-drink business clean-water expertise to the city's needs. The removal of the old Central Market, another of Vernor's causes, further modernized Detroit by allowing for expansion of its business center.

Of course, financing all of these improvements for the city and its people required taxation. Fortunately the tax base continued to grow, but Vernor was not opposed to raising taxes for a reasonable cause such as education or improvement to infrastructure. He said that taxes "are unpleasant but necessary for obtaining desired benefits. I am of the opinion that taxpayers are not quite so much concerned about the amount of taxes as they are concerned about resulting benefits. Money properly expended is never wasted."[13]

In a reelection bid in 1921 Vernor was a strong advocate of education and was called the "Father of Civil Service" for supporting laws to reform the civil service. City workers up to that time had been mostly political appointees, serving at the whim of the current political machine. After the reforms, these workers would be secure in their positions only as long as they performed their jobs adequately. Vernor also helped raise the salaries of the city's teachers, seeing that attracting and retaining good teachers required competing with the industries growing in the city. Besides helping secure property for new school buildings as Detroit's population expanded, Vernor supported a compulsory education law that required students to stay in school until the age of eighteen. He had originally opposed compulsory education

> *"I am a Red Wings fanatic. Raised in Detroit, there is nothing better than sitting down to watch a hockey game on TV with a Vernor's in hand. Except being there!"*
> —Kim Delmar Cory

A Vernor's invoice from 1897, signed "James Vernor, Jr."

because it left no room for the possibility of a student having to go to work full-time to support a family that may have lost its primary breadwinner. He changed his mind when a form of relief for the poor became available in the city. To recognize his support of educational issues, an elementary school in Detroit was named in his honor.

Vernor's political career was not uncomplicated or selfless, and some of his decisions and uses of influence on the common council appear to have been motivated by his own personal financial interests and those of his friends. One example occurred in 1915 when a proposal came before the council to establish a municipal ferry service to Belle Isle and Windsor, Ontario, across the Detroit River. The proposal put the terminal at the foot of First Street and would have routed foot traffic off Woodward Avenue and away from Vernor's retail store.[14] Vernor managed to kill this proposal, arguing that the proposed development was illegal. When this same proposal came before council a second time with the support of the city attorney and many others, Vernor led a coalition to defeat it again. Eventually a ferry service to Windsor was established at the foot of Woodward, which was more conducive to increased traffic past Vernor's store.

Another proposal brought before the council called for the building of a subway under Woodward Avenue. Vernor applauded this idea until it transpired that a station would have to be built in front of his store, thereby blocking access to the store and the view of potential customers from the street as well. That was the end of his support for this project, which fizzled.

Another ferry service established much later at the foot of Woodward Avenue and situated right across from the Vernor's plant and retail outlet proved to be a boon for the sale of Vernor's Ginger Ale. The ferry to Bob-Lo Island helped to establish Vernor's as Detroit's Drink, as thousands stopped in before boarding for a cool draught of ginger ale or a Boston cooler, which combined ginger ale with ice cream. Vernor had no objections to this ferry.

Oh yeah, that's a Detroit original. I was 20 when I first came to Michigan, and people were surprised that I already liked Vernor's. They thought no one outside of Michigan had heard of it. But it was popular in LA, where I grew up.
—Michael

Around this time, a proposal was introduced that businesses using space under the streets of Detroit be charged rent for that space by the city. Upon discovering that this would have cost the Vernor's Company $700 in rent per year to store the aging barrels, Vernor used his influence to beat down this proposal as well. Detroiters were noticing an apparent pattern of conflict of interest, which almost cost Vernor his reputation and seat on the council.

In late 1921, Mayor James Couzens pushed for a recall of Vernor, accusing him of conflict of interest in owning stock in the Detroit Edison Company, the electrical utility. Couzens claimed that this violated the city charter, which prohibited any council

The old plant on the Detroit River with the Windsor ferry
and the Bob-Lo Island ferry at their docks

member from voting on any question in which he was financially
interested. The feisty Vernor retorted, "[the] mayor may find that
someone else can circulate recall petitions as well as he can. . . .
Mr. Couzens' connection with Bank of Detroit, which handles city
funds, is equally as illegal."[15] In retrospect this apparent conflict of
interest cast a shadow on Vernor's political career, but no formal
action came of it.

Vernor remained in elected office until 1924 and stayed
active in politics and civic service well into his 80s. He was often
encouraged to run for mayor but always declined. Detroit's
Vernor Highway was named in his honor for his many years of
service to the city.

Founding Father of Detroit's Drink **21**

Detroit's Pop Boom Years

From the late 1800s to the early 1900s the United States experienced tremendous growth that brought increased wages, more disposable income, and shorter working days. Industry's promise of leisure and luxury was nowhere more evident than in Detroit. Not too many miles from Vernor's operation, in Highland Park, Henry Ford had started production of the Model T and revolutionized manufacturing with the moving assembly line. The "Motor City" soon attracted seekers of high-paying jobs at the many automobile companies and suppliers springing up around the city. Ford turned the manufacturing world upside down in 1913 with his offer of five dollars a day,

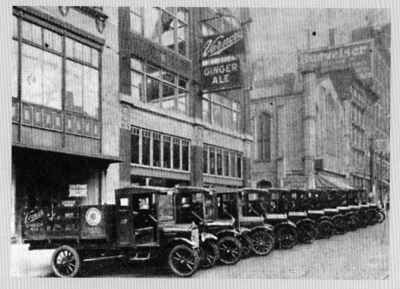

An early Vernor's delivery fleet

wages unheard of by the average worker then. This shrewd tactic
enabled the workers to afford the cars they built and much more
besides, and demand for consumer goods boomed in Detroit as
industrial advances made new variety and convenience possible.
For example, by 1904, Michael Owens in nearby Toledo
had perfected and patented his completely automated bottle-
manufacturing machine, making reliable bottles cheap to produce,
and Baltimore inventor William Painter's crimped crown cap
solved the sealing problem.

The Vernors expanded their retail outlet at the corner
of Woodward and Woodbridge in 1906 and again in 1918.
Thousands of Detroiters refreshed themselves at Vernor's elaborate fountain counter before boarding the ferries to Belle Isle and
Windsor. By 1915 the operation was incorporated, full-time, and
large in scope. American distribution had reached Toledo,

**The retail shop at the foot of Woodward,
on the way to the Bob-Lo Island ferry**
Courtesy of Joan and Darrell Lissolo

Cleveland, and Buffalo. Vernor's also went international around
this time with exports to Windsor and Toronto.

The Vernors continued to pursue stringent quality control
with their own water purification plant, carbonic gas production, and high standards for ingredients, such as ginger imported
from Jamaica. These strict controls assured Vernor's continuing
popularity through product consistency and customer loyalty,
and the closely guarded secret formula guaranteed a fresh, gingery taste competitors could not duplicate. (The two Vernors
kept the recipe to themselves, delegating purchasing of different
ingredients to different people so that no one but the Vernors

knew every ingredient of the base syrup.) By this time, any self-respecting soda fountain in the city was dispensing Vernor's, and thirsty households consumed thousands of cases of bottles. Hospitals were another successful market for Vernor's Ginger Ale, well known for soothing the stomach. Anyone who grew up in Detroit around this time was sure to get a glass of Vernor's to treat childhood illnesses at some point. Because of the increased demand, by 1916 the Vernor's Detroit delivery fleet consisted of eight Model T Ford stake-bed trucks, each able to carry seventy cases of ginger ale bottles.

After World War I the end of the war's hardships and sugar shortages and the growth of the temperance movement greatly invigorated the soft-drink industry. Michigan had become a dry state on May 1, 1917, but it would be another three years before Prohibition would become a national policy. (Michigan had actually tried Prohibition as early as 1855, but repealed this ineffectual law by 1875.) The sale of Vernor's Ginger Ale in the Detroit area increased during this period as law-abiding citizens sought alternatives to alcohol.

By this time the firm was ready to expand again, so the company bought an old power plant at the foot of Woodward Avenue by the Detroit River. This building soon grew by six stories, and the Vernors began supplying franchises with the syrup instead of making the finished soda only at the main plant. The building became a landmark on the waterfront, known by the huge Vernor's logo painted on the side facing the river. With the bottling business well established, James Vernor II took an interest in public affairs much as his father had before him. The elder Vernor's civic activities had long kept him away from the business most of the time, but the two kept an office with adjacent desks for over thirty years.

On October 28, 1919, Congress passed the National Prohibition Act (also known as the Volstead Act) to enforce the recently ratified Eighteenth Amendment prohibiting the manufacture and sale of alcoholic beverages. Prohibition would last only until 1933, but it triggered a boom in the consumption of soft drinks as the supply of booze dwindled. This also opened the door for more family-oriented soda fountain operations as corner saloons disappeared. Detroit became a major center of bootlegging, being near liquor-tolerant Canada. Many boatloads of illicit liquor crossed the Detroit River under cover of darkness. Even as the absence of legal liquor drove up demand for soft drinks, the bad flavor of many of the illegal alternatives helped make soft drinks popular as mixers.

Some breweries converted to the production of root beer and near-beer (a nonalcoholic beer) to try to stay in business, but these attempts usually failed, as did many of the breweries themselves. The most famous brewery in Detroit was the Stroh Brewery Company, established in 1850, which also had to innovate to survive the new law. Stroh had converted part of its production to a nonalcoholic beer to supply its in-state clientele after Michigan voted itself dry in 1916. The new product's unenticing name, Temperance Beer, was soon changed to Stroh's Bohemian Style Lager. The legal alcohol limit for such beverages was 0.5 percent. These near-beers were not a hit, but brewers were hopeful that Prohibition could not last.

> Vernor's, my favorite! When we were sick as kids my dad would give us flat Vernor's so we would not get dehydrated. It isn't as "gingery" as it once was but I still love it. It has such a distinctive taste. . . . I once went to the Vernor's plant in Detroit and had an ice cream float. The best ever.
> —Anne

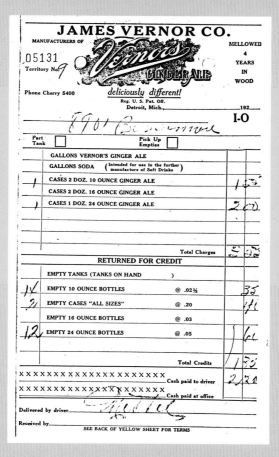

An invoice from the 1920s shows a 24-bottle case of
10-ounce bottles with a wholesale price of $1.25
and a case of 24-ounce bottles for $2.00.

The solution for the Stroh Company was soft drinks and ice
cream. Bottling and production equipment and a distribution
network were already in place to launch Birch Beer, a kind of
root beer, along with other flavors including orange, cola, club
soda, and Caledonia Dry Ginger Ale, a competitor of Canada
Dry Ginger Ale more than of Vernor's. Soft drinks were a stopgap
measure for Stroh, however, and their Alaska brand ice cream

REMEMBER
TO SER~ VERNOR'S GINGER ALE PROPERLY ~ MUST BE
ICE COLD

BOTTLES

TERMS NET CASH — NO DISCOUNT.

It is understood and mutually agreed by the manufacturer and customer that the bottles and cases in which the merchandise sold is contained, are not sold to the customer, but always remain the property of the manufacturer, and that the customer has no right to dispose of said bottles or cases in any manner whatsoever, and—

It is further understood and mutually agreed that the deposit taken by the manufacturer is not to be considered as payment or part payment for the said cases and bottles, but merely as a guarantee that said cases and bottles will be returned to the manufacturer, at which time the deposit will be refunded; and the manufacturer shall, in the event that the customer fails or refuses to return the cases and bottles, charge against and collect from the customer the value of any and all shortages in the return of said bottles and cases, and in such event shall give the customer credit for his deposit against such charge.

TANKS

TERMS NET CASH — NO DISCOUNT.

All tank goods are sold under the following conditions:

That all tanks are to be considered as loaned property only.

That the length of time a customer is to keep a tank is not to exceed 30 days.

That at the expiration of 30 days tanks are to be picked up, and in the event of their not being empty, no credit is to be allowed.

Where carbonator or charging apparatus is installed, the length of time a tank of soda may be kept by customer is 10 days. Same to be picked up at that time and no credit allowed in event of not being empty.

That all tanks are to be kept inside of building until picked up by our driver. If stolen or damaged by fire while in your possession you are held responsible.

In order to give prompt service we must have your co-operation in the way of returning promptly all tanks, bottles and cases. Tell our driver or office about these.

Inform us also of any inattention on the part of our employees. Our aim is "A high standard product and prompt service."

JAMES VERNOR CO.

Phone Cherry 5400   239 Woodward Ave.

THIS IS YOUR INVOICE — Keep It

THE SHELBY SALESBOOK CO., SHELBY, OHIO   53-936

The back of the invoice, outlining the terms of sale

was the only nonalcoholic product whose production continued after the repeal of the Volstead Act, when Stroh returned to brewing beer. Stroh also produced a hopped malt syrup sold and advertised as a candy and baking ingredient but also discreetly described as useful in "beverages." (The home brewers avoided prosecution under the new law as long as they did not sell their product.) These products helped Stroh survive the thirteen-year dry spell to become the nation's third largest brewer.[16]

Ginger ale was a favored mixer, and sales of Vernor's contin-

Vernors I, II, and III
Courtesy of the Detroit Public Library

ued to rise, but able competitors vied for the mixer market. It all started in the late 1800s in Toronto, where pharmacist John James McLaughlin had been experimenting with flavorings for the local soft-drink industry. The pale, dry ginger ale he developed, McLaughlin's Belfast Style Ginger Ale, was popular in the late 1890s. A later refinement sold under the name McLaughlin's Pale Dry Ginger Ale, but in 1905 McLaughlin settled on Canada Dry Pale Ginger Ale. Like Vernor, McLaughlin was also a stickler for quality, purity, and consistency, which explains his product's survival. Exported to the United States a few years later, Canada Dry Ginger Ale became a popular mixer, which was never the case with Vernor's due to its strong taste. Canada Dry's subtler,

James Vernor, "the Boss," presented with a cake by his adoring employees in 1927. A photograph of the first James Vernor can be seen over a worker's head in the background.

less vivid flavor made it more compatible with some liquors. Some Detroiters came to prefer this milder ginger ale, but many remained loyal to their familiar extra-spicy, extra-bubbly Vernor's.

James Vernor died late in 1927 at age eighty-four, leaving behind not just a successful company but also great civic accomplishments in his hometown of Detroit. The mayor of Detroit at the time of Vernor's death, John W. Smith, said that Vernor's "long public service and his kindly disposition endeared him to all . . . . [James Vernor's] place in Detroit will never be filled."[17]

As he proved during his career, James Vernor II inherited his father's drive, integrity, and business sense. The younger Vernor had big shoes to fill, but he was up to the challenges before him. The golden era of Vernor's Ginger Ale was about to start.

James Vernor II continued to expand the company's distribu-

One of the original promotional trucks
that appeared at events around the city

tion and marketing. The newly expanded plant, with over 50,000 square feet of floor space, represented the state of the art for the industry. Bottles and cases returned to the plant went for inspection to the top floor, where broken bottles were discarded and wooden cases repaired or replaced. They then descended through the cleaning and refilling process to arrive at ground level, ready to ship.

After the extract, the plant's water purification system was probably the most critical element to the product's success. To meet Vernor's standards, water had to pass through six cleansing stages: a series of electrical plates to kill microorganisms, then tank storage to allow sedimentation of solids, then a five-foot-thick quartz filter, then charcoal filters, then ultraviolet light. Finally the pure, sterile water flowed at high pressure through a paper filter, which was inspected daily as a check on the other filters.[18] This system, which the Vernors once even had tested with

The old Woodward Avenue plant sometime in the early 1940s. The sign with the pouring bottle would inspire the design for the famous sign at the new plant farther north up Woodward.

lethal typhoid bacilli (none of which made it through), produced about seventy-two thousand gallons of purified water per day.

The reusable bottles went through similarly careful inspection and cleaning. Once the bottles entered the washing process, through the final rinse with sterilized water produced by the plant, and until filling and sealing at the end of the line, no human hands touched them. A pressure test before filling that exploded any flawed or weak ones guaranteed the bottles' integrity. After filling, a final inspection hunted down any leaky caps before the cases rolled along the conveyor to the loading dock and delivery trucks. This process could produce sixty thousand bottles a day. The fountain service multiplied the actual output of ginger ale many times over.

> *... Texas is home for now. I thought this was the last place in the country I'd ever live—and the funny thing is, it just may be. I like it here in Austin. Plenty of good people, food, and beer to keep me happy. Send me a six-pack of Vernor's and I'm sure it'll all be OK.*
> —Bill Sodeman

Vernor II also streamlined the company's office paperwork. The *Credit Digest* praised the company for installing the latest automated accounting system "with the result that five or six girls easily compile records that formerly necessitated the work of thirty-five or more clerks."[19] The Vernors spared no effort or rigor to become a leader in the industry. That Vernor's Ginger Ale never matched the popularity of Canada Dry, Coca-Cola, Pepsi-Cola, or even Dr Pepper may be because, as with licorice or sauternes, the taste for its delicious difference is one that not everyone can acquire.

Another Detroit competitor of Vernor's also ended up dwarfed by the big soft-drink companies, but this competitor reached a degree of success that Vernor's never attained. This company was started in 1907 by two Russian immigrant brothers, Perry and Benjamin Feigenson, who called their business Faygo. This small soft-drink business also grew from humble beginnings and included sons who joined the family endeavor. In 1935, Faygo opened a large manufacturing facility on Gratiot Avenue, near the Vernor's plant. They were not blessed with the ideal location that Vernor's enjoyed for retail sales, but instead relied heavily on advertising and mass marketing, quickly capturing a thirty-state market. Their product line was more diverse, with root beer, orange soda, and various fruit flavors, one of which was later marketed with the clever name of Red Pop. One of the most unique Faygo flavors, still popular today, is Rock and Rye,

The rotating bottle-filling line

reportedly named for a Prohibition-era drink made of rye whiskey and a cube, or "rock," of sugar.

The Feigensons had a genius for marketing, getting out the message that drinking Faygo was a fun, youthful activity. The family members were also devoted baseball fans, and Faygo was well known for sponsoring the beloved Detroit Tigers baseball team. Faygo enjoyed great success and became a symbol of Detroit much like Vernor's, and the two companies dominated the Detroit soft-drink market in the early decades of the twentieth century.

After the stock market crash of 1929 many of the smaller soft drink companies failed. Even Pepsi-Cola fell into bankruptcy in May 1931. Although soft drinks were a low-cost consumer good, they were an expendable luxury to those facing hard times. Soft-drink sales continued to decline during the Depression, reaching

James Vernor Davis

their lowest point sometime in 1932, when total production of soft drinks in the U.S. reached barely 1.4 million cases. Another blow to the industry was a reinstated federal excise tax on syrup and carbonic gas. This tax had first appeared during World War I but ended with the conclusion of the war. After the tax's reinstatement for two years beginning in 1932, competition in the industry intensified as producers struggled to survive under this additional financial burden. Another development in the 1930s was the introduction of the twelve-ounce bottle, most notably by Pepsi, who advertised the new size at the old eight-ounce price of only a nickel. This maneuver pressured the competition to react with new, larger sizes at the same price, and some brands even offered sixteen ounces for a nickel. The strong emerged stronger from this trying period.

Although Vernor's balance sheet during this time must have

A Vernor's delivery truck typical of the era. Vernor's trucks were easily recognized by their striking green- and gold-painted designs.

reflected the decrease in consumer spending, the company weathered the storm just as it had during the war years, thanks to its good management and basic financial strength. Some Depression-era relief may have come from the 1929 opening of the Ambassador Bridge not far from the Vernor's plant. This linked Detroit with its Canadian neighbors in Windsor, enhancing the transport of goods and encouraging commerce across the international border.

In 1931 Vernor I's nephew, James Vernor Davis, joined the company. The family firm was now achieving annual sales of $2.25 million (compared with $10,000 in 1897). Davis oversaw a rapid proliferation of Vernor's plants around the country during his tenure, but during the Depression years the company faced serious labor issues.

In December 1935, the company faced a labor dispute and lawsuit over the firing of twenty-three delivery drivers a few months earlier.[20] The company claimed that the National Labor Relations

Board had no jurisdiction in the case as outlined by the Wagner Act. Labor unions in Detroit were growing more powerful and aggressive, especially in the automobile companies. Like many other Detroit companies, Vernor's would not escape labor unrest and unionization.

By 1936 Vernor's Ginger Ale was for sale in more than forty thousand locations in the Midwest and Canada, nine thousand of which were in the Detroit area, and the company was contributing more than $400,000 in wages to the economy per year. Seventy trucks were needed just to service the Detroit area, and two million gallons of Vernor's were required to meet the demand that year. Branch plants operated in additional Michigan cities (Ann Arbor, Flint, Jackson, Pontiac, Port Huron, and Saginaw), in Ohio (Cincinnati, Cleveland, Dayton, and Toledo), in New York State (Buffalo and Niagara Falls), and in Walkerville, Ontario.[21] The company had also introduced two new products, Arcadia Dry Ginger Ale and Arcadia Sparkling Water, meant to compete with Canada Dry and marketed as mixers. The sparkling water was simply the pure filtered water that the company already produced, carbonated and bottled. Logical extensions of the product line though they seemed to be, these offerings lasted only a few years before being withdrawn, having never met the marketplace challenge of Canada Dry.

The seventieth anniversary celebration of the company in July 1936 at the Woodward Avenue Plant included free Vernor's Ginger Ale for all who showed up. According to a *Detroit News* story, Vernor's gave away more than 100,000 glasses by 11:30 A.M.[22] Hundreds had lined up at the door for the early morning opening. John W. Smith, on behalf of Mayor Frank Couzens, visited the celebration at noon along with members of the Detroit City Council to present the city's official congratulations.

"A double-layer cake was the gift of the Hotel Statler while the Book-Cadillac sent a fifty-pound sponge layer cake."[23] The *News* reported that one of the highlights of the day was a visit by a seventy-five-year-old woman, Mrs. Margaret Bene Lefferts, who traveled alone by streetcar to attend. She recounted walking to the original drugstore from her home near what is now Glendale and Twelfth. Lefferts said to Vernor II, "After I had finished my glass your father used to give me another one free. He was a fine man and you look like one too. But you haven't the fine mustache your father had." Vernor's kept giving away free ginger ale at every company celebration until the 1960s.

I used to live in South Florida in the sixties. My dad had a little grocery store on 17th Avenue near Coral Gables. He sold Vernor's, and it was pretty popular! I guess all the snowbirds from Michigan started the trend down there as we used to see a lot of Michigan tags in the winter.
—June

As the Vernor's company began to make expansive franchising plans, they also made plans to increase local production with the purchase of the old Siegal building, a Detroit landmark that had housed a women's clothing store. By 1941 the "Most Modern Bottling Facility in the World" was ready to open, designed by architects Harley and Ellington and constructed by H. B. Culbertson. The plant now occupied an entire city block that was dubbed the "Vernor Block," bounded by Woodward, Atwater, Griswold, and Woodbridge. The public was again treated to free Vernor's at the grand opening celebration on June 18, 1941. At the huge party in the Crystal Ballroom of the Hotel Book-Cadillac, "all the invited guests were native Detroiters, 75 years of age or older, and the presidents of business houses established at least by 1866."[24]

The party honored many Detroiters along with Davis, Emily

Vernor Leonard, Vernor II, and his son, young Lieutenant James
Vernor III, who had joined the army and reported to Fort
Sheridan, Illinois, with the 210th Coast Artillery, Anti-Aircraft
Division.[25] (James Vernor IV was still a baby.) Dancing and mer-
riment continued through the night, with dance demonstrations
by Arthur Murray Dance Studios students under the direction of
Benjamin B. Lovett, dance master for Henry Ford. James Vernor III
had attended Culver Military Academy in Indiana and graduated
second in his class in 1937. He attended Michigan State College
(now University) in East Lansing for two years before joining the
army. His college career appeared to be undistinguished except by
his reputation as a drinker and debauchee, but upon entering the
army he was recruited for officer training because of his previous
military training at Culver. He later went to the Aleutian Islands
of Alaska, where he served with merit, and he returned from
the war a lieutenant colonel. He and his wife, Grayce Stoddard
Vernon, had two children, James
IV in 1940 and Grayce in
1941. James Vernor IV
followed his father's
footsteps to Culver
Military Academy and
today is a stockbroker
in Birmingham, Michigan,
with offices on North Woodward
Avenue, not far from the original home of
Vernor's Ginger Ale. James Vernor V and James Vernor VI both live
in Minnesota. Grayce Vernor Shannon lives in South Carolina.

World War II was not the best time to be in the soft-drink
business, as rationing limited such essential supplies as gasoline

*Green is one of my
favorite colors; maybe it goes
back to when I was five and my dad
(a sign painter) painted my first drawing
desk Vernor's green from left-over paint from
a Vernor's job. My dad's sign shop was on
Gratiot Road, St. Clair, Michigan. By the
way, Vernor's is my favorite drink.
—Phil Pegg*

James Vernor II with the seventy-fifth
anniversary cake at the Hotel Book-Cadillac

for delivery trucks and sugar for the ginger ale. Even rubber
for tires and metal used in bottle caps were being diverted to
defense. Many manufacturers switched to high-fructose corn
syrup as rationing reduced the sugar supply. Some tried a new
artificial sweetener, saccharin, but many states had banned it for
problems then attributed to it besides its unpleasant flavor. Some
soft-drink manufacturers, such as Coca-Cola and Pepsi-Cola,

began recycling old bottle caps, setting up collection containers at points of purchase. As the country concentrated on winning the war, Vernor's operated with reduced manpower and tight supplies.

After the war, a new prosperity took hold in Detroit as the automobile companies strove to meet the demand pent up by wartime restrictions on car production for civilians. Vernor III returned from the war to work in the plant. As demand for Vernor's Ginger Ale increased along with the postwar demand for most goods, a Vernor's franchise became a viable business opportunity. The franchise booklet published by Vernor's in 1944 suggests that a franchisee in a town of one to three hundred

> *I grew up in Michigan waaaaayyy back when Vernor's ginger ale was still made in a small factory run by a local family in Detroit. Michiganders from the '50's–'60's like myself remember that the only thing to drink when not feeling well was Vernor's (aged in oak barrels) because it worked. Its flavor came to be associated with "feel good, feel better," that kind of thing. Used to make ice cream floats . . . aaah, the best!*
> *—Barbara B.*

thousand invest $5,000 for machinery and equipment, $6,000 for bottles and cases, $4,800 for four trucks, and a deferred payment of $10,000 to Vernor's. It suggests a yearly payroll of $13,300 for a staff and yearly operating expenses of $22,790. The cost of producing a case of eight-ounce bottles of Vernor's Ginger Ale was $0.29, and their wholesale price was $0.80. Vernor's franchises were awarded for a thirty-year period in an exclusive territory. For every gallon of extract purchased by the franchisee, the company added a $4.00 credit to an account applicable toward point-of-purchase displays and metal signs. Franchisees had to pay for any other advertising, but Vernor's would supply copy and illustrations at no cost.

In 1951, the city of Detroit asked Vernor's to make way for a new convention and civic center planned for the riverfront. Its

The new plant at 4501 Woodward Avenue around 1960

centerpiece would be Cobo Hall, a convention center to replace
the older one a few miles north on Woodward Avenue near
Wayne State University and an area known as the cultural center.
The city proposed 4501 Woodward Avenue, the site of the old
convention center, as the new location of Vernor's. A deal was
struck, the city issued a condemnation on September 22, 1951,
and Vernor's moved again. Vernor III said, "I certainly couldn't
stand in the way of progress."[26] The old plant would have to be
razed, and the new site needed thorough renovation to suit the
company's needs. This presented the opportunity for Vernor's
once again to build a showplace state-of-the-art manufacturing
plant.

The cost of renovating and removing to the new site was over $5 million. Although the new building was three thousand square feet larger than the old location, it was long and flat, requiring abandonment of the vertically oriented operations at the old plant, which used gravity to move things. The new building was two floors above street level and had about eleven acres of floor space on a seven-acre site, fronting a long stretch of Woodward Avenue. This configuration allowed the installation of glass along the whole Woodward Avenue side of the building, to showcase the cleanliness and efficiency of the operation and attract passersby to the modern retail soda fountain inside.

The four nearly completely automated lines could produce six million six-ounce portions in twenty-four hours.[27] This is about 750 cases per line, per hour (or enough to supply two servings a day for everyone in the metropolitan Detroit area, as the *Detroit News* expressed it). Vernor's had nine other plants around the country and many franchises, and the new plant was to supply the base syrup for all of these. Even the loading and unloading of the trucks was mechanized. According to James E. Briggs, the chief engineer at the time, the plant would require enough electrical power to supply a small city with its more than two hundred electric motors, air conditioning, and modern lighting.

The plans for the new plant continued as the old plant prepared for the eighty-fifth anniversary party to be held on June 18, 1951. These parties had become a birthday tradition in Detroit. The years of hard work and dedication were starting to show on the 74-year-old elder Vernor, and he was again facing a major transition. By this time Vernor II was serving as chairman of the board and Vernor III was executive vice president. A full-page ad appearing in the Detroit papers announced the open house celebration and showed four generations of the family, including James Vernor IV. J. Vernor Davis, not pictured, was waiting in the wings to be appointed president the next year.

The new plant officially opened at 4501 Woodward Avenue on June 30, 1954, marking the seventh corporate move for Vernor's. Unfortunately James Vernor II did not live to see his work come to fruition; "the Boss" died of cancer on April 11, 1954. This ended an era, and the Vernor's Company would hardly be recognizable a decade later.

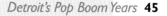

Modernization

The new bottling plant was a strikingly modern model of automation, efficiency, and cleanliness. Competitors came to tour it, and passersby on Woodward Avenue saw nearly every step in Vernor's operations through the windows. Enameled metal panels in the familiar gold and green flanked the glass, which had a gleaming stainless steel border. The terrazzo tile lobby floor depicted the Vernor's gnome, the popular company mascot. The plant was opulent and stylish in every way, even down to its sleek offices

A former Woodward Avenue landmark, the animated gnome pouring ginger ale

finished in Philippine mahogany. An unforgettable sign stood fifty-five feet tall outside the south end of the building, glowing with 75,000 watts of neon light as the mirthful gnome poured a glass of ginger ale every five seconds. That glittering sign, evoking the effervescent bubbles of Vernor's, is a fond memory to many who grew up in midcentury Detroit.

The new bottling plant operated over a mile of conveyors, using both power and gravity, through meticulously sanitized equipment, much of it custom designed for the plant. In the syrup room, four three-hundred-gallon stainless steel tanks cooked the initial sugar mixture, which then flowed through a cooling system and into a mixing room to meet the aged extract syrup and the purified water. The final mixing room contained six three-hundred-gallon mixing tanks and four one-thousand-gallon storage tanks. This entire process was automatic (except for the initial manual loading of the sugar) and controlled by a single instrument panel.

The bottling line at the new plant

The bottling line being installed

View from Woodward Avenue *(left)* and interior

The water purification system resembled that of the old plant, with three five-thousand-gallon settling tanks; twelve sand, gravel, and activated carbon filters; six water polishers; and three ultraviolet treatment machines. Twelve electrolysis devices were a novel improvement in this new system, which produced fifteen thousand gallons per hour for the ginger ale and the final bottle rinse.

The new plant produced ginger ale in eight- and twenty-four-ounce bottles, ten-gallon tanks for commercial use, and ten-gallon home-service fountain tanks. These home kegs of ginger ale, available for parties or other large and thirsty events, were unique in the industry. A case of eight-ounce bottles retailed for $1.12, and eight-ounce glasses at the fountain were a dime. In contrast with the plant's automation and efficiencies, the highly concentrated extract syrup was still aged over four years in wooden barrels. The plant also produced gallon containers of this potent stuff for shipment to the other plants and franchises, where it was mixed at one part to seven hundred.

Barrels of extract syrup in the aging room

Section of the network of conveyors

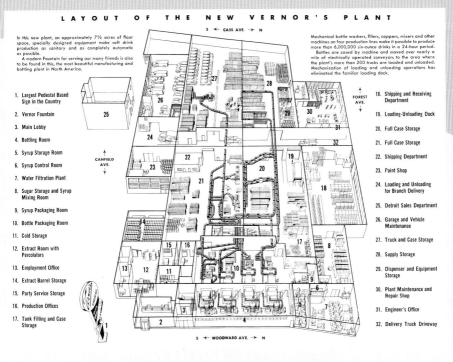

S ← CASS AVE. → N

In this new plant, on approximately 7½ acres of floor space, specially designed equipment make soft drink production as sanitary and as completely automatic as possible.

A modern Fountain for serving our many friends is also to be found in this, the most beautiful manufacturing and bottling plant in North America.

Mechanical bottle washers, fillers, cappers, mixers and other machines on four production lines make it possible to produce more than 6,000,000 six-ounce drinks in a 24-hour period.

Bottles are cased by machine and moved over nearly a mile of electrically operated conveyors to the area where the plant's more than 200 trucks are loaded and unloaded. Mechanization of loading and unloading operations has eliminated the familiar loading dock.

1. Largest Pedestal Based Sign in the Country
2. Vernor Fountain
3. Main Lobby
4. Bottling Room
5. Syrup Storage Room
6. Syrup Control Room
7. Water Filtration Plant
8. Sugar Storage and Syrup Mixing Room
9. Syrup Packaging Room
10. Bottle Packaging Room
11. Cold Storage
12. Extract Room with Percolators
13. Employment Office
14. Extract Barrel Storage
15. Party Service Storage
16. Production Offices
17. Tank Filling and Case Storage

18. Shipping and Receiving Department
19. Loading-Unloading Dock
20. Full Case Storage
21. Full Case Storage
22. Shipping Department
23. Paint Shop
24. Loading and Unloading for Branch Delivery
25. Detroit Sales Department
26. Garage and Vehicle Maintenance
27. Truck and Case Storage
28. Supply Storage
29. Dispenser and Equipment Storage
30. Plant Maintenance and Repair Shop
31. Engineer's Office
32. Delivery Truck Driveway

CANFIELD AVE.

FOREST AVE.

S ← WOODWARD AVE. → N

Floor plan for the production line

The delivery fleet also improved, adding forty-nine new trucks with custom-built Herman Low-Boy bodies that carried 350 cases of ginger ale. The whole fleet by this time consisted of about 350 vehicles made by Ford, Chevrolet, Dodge, White, and others. Four White, two Ford, six GMC, and three International tractors pulled twelve Fruehauf forty-foot trailers, each capable of carrying 1,048 cases. Nine Chevrolet sedan-delivery trucks, featuring the familiar green and gold color scheme and a new embellishment, the jolly gnome image, made the rounds of promotional opportunities.

A Ford tractor-trailer combination from the 1950s

With the new plant in full operation, James Vernor Davis could attend to expanding sales and marketing. The company had seen continuing production increases and sales success under his and Jim Vernor III's leadership. Jim Vernor III died on April 11, 1957. He was only thirty-nine, but heavy alcohol use had brought on cirrhosis.[28] The estate of James Vernor II remained unsettled, and the family faced additional inheritance tax problems upon Vernor III's death. In need of cash, they made plans to take the company public. During this period the apostrophe disappeared from the company's name. The Vernor family continued to hold a significant number of shares but not for long.

By 1962 Vernor's was no longer a closely held family firm. Over two thousand shareholders from twenty-five states and Canada held stock in the company, owning a total of half a million shares out of an authorized seven hundred thousand shares. Net sales in the early sixties were stagnant. Some of the company's sales problems came from increasingly aggressive marketing from other soft-drink companies with larger resources. Americans had also become more health-conscious and were shying away from high-calorie beverages. Vernor's responded with the introduction of

1950s Chevrolet stake-bed truck for local delivery

Vernor's 1-Calorie in June 1962, which brought some fizz back into their sales figures.

When Vernor's 1-Calorie first appeared in Michigan in the twelve-ounce can, sales exceeded expectations, reaching over three hundred thousand cases during the four-month introductory period. This was more than twice the national sales rate of sugar-free soft drinks. Although this was only a small percentage of overall sales, it spurred the company to introduce the product to the entire Vernor's distribution area.

Concerned with lagging sales overall, Davis ordered a reorganization of the sales department in 1962. Sales increased, and some of the branch locations converted to franchise opera-

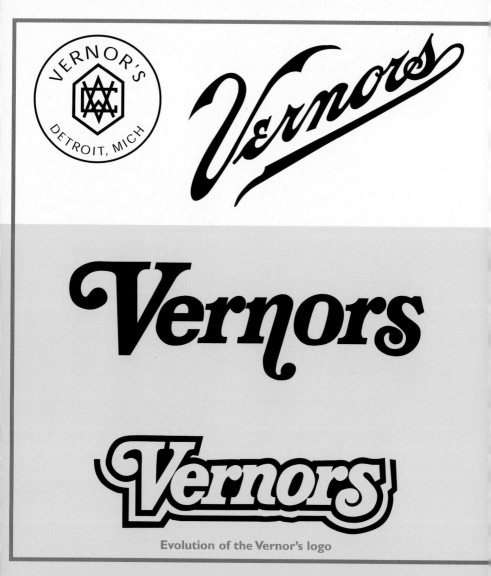

Evolution of the Vernor's logo

tions, improving the parent company's bottom line. The company worked to increase the number of franchise operators and applied to Vernor's Ginger Ale the marketing techniques learned from the introduction of 1-Calorie and from competitors. By 1963, as sales hit an all-time high, earnings were up 20 percent

and an extra dividend paid. The company entered into an agree-
ment with Continental Beverages Limited of Montreal to franchise bottling operations throughout the home turf of Canada
Dry. More company-held American operations were converted to
franchisees at the same time. Franchises had become much more

important to the company, contributing one-third of income in 1963, compared to only about 3 percent ten years earlier. The company ended 1963 in the strongest financial position in its almost 100-year history.

The Vernor's business strategy of the era included distributing other products, which by 1962 included RC Cola, Hires Root Beer, Orange Crush, Diet-Rite Cola, and Mason's Root Beer in selected franchised territories. In 1963, Squirt joined the line-up, and in 1964 Vernor's 1-Calorie and Diet-Rite Cola appeared in bottles for the first time. This effort and increases in the cost of sugar at the beginning of the year hurt earnings. Sales in the Detroit territory had surprisingly started to lag, resulting in a reorganization of that department. The slump in sales around Detroit resulted in a disappointing 1965, with only $9.3 million in revenue and net earnings per share down to $0.36. A strike at the Detroit plant further reduced third-quarter earnings, not the last time that labor unrest would plague the company. That year's unusually cold summer may also have hurt sales. In October, the company invested in introducing Vernor's in cans to the metropolitan New York City market.

In June of 1966, Vernor's celebrated its centennial with the usual birthday fanfare, despite a sad

> Now I have to figure out if that ginger ale was invented by someone named Vernor (therefore it is Vernor's Ginger Ale) or by somebody named Vernors or by somebody named Vernor and the usage just got corrupted to Vernors. I know someone who uses "mines" when describing something that belongs to him. Meanwhile, would youse like to order now? Or is it "Come on, youse guys, let's play hockey, eh!"
> —Kerry Irons

change in circumstances. Several months before, the company had been sold to a group of institutional investors led by Cyrus J. Lawrence & Sons, members of the New York Stock Exchange, for around $4.5 million.[29] The family had to divest themselves of the company to meet tax liabilities reaching back to the death of James Vernor II.[30] Along with the new owners came plans for major changes. Production, sales, advertising, public relations, and franchise operations all came under scrutiny. The old Vernor's was gone forever.

The family business had outgrown the family. James Vernor Davis moved from president to chairman of the board as outsiders took over production and marketing. Professional managers came in to transform operations and the company's culture in the first of many corporate restructuring schemes. Vernor's was surviving the soft-drink wars at the cost of changing from intimate family business to impersonal corporate entity.

Frank's Foods took control of a majority interest in Vernor's in 1971 and in 1972 was in turn acquired by American Consumer Products. The 1973 line-up included (in addition to the regular Vernor's products)

> *They may have shamed me into saying "soda," but they can't change what's in my heart. Mmmm ... makes me want a nice cold can of Vernor's ... the best pop in the world.*
> *—Melinda J. Beasi*

Flier sent to franchisees to promote the release of Vernor's 1-Calorie

fruit colas, Royal Crown Cola, Nestea, Weight Watchers drinks, and Gatorade. Vernor's sold these products mainly in Michigan through franchises and did not manufacture them. By 1976, Vernor's was sold as far west as Los Angeles, as far south as Florida (where vacationing snow-weary Detroiters had helped make it popular), north into Canada, and east into New York State, but much of the west and other regions of the country remained virgin territory. Locally Vernor's arranged with another Detroit company, Sanders (whose hot fudge sauce still enjoys a

From a centennial promotional calendar

cult following much like Vernor's), to produce Vernor's Ice Cream. Vernor's supplied their extract syrup and Sanders made the ice cream, a relationship that lasted only a few years, though it seemed natural enough. (People still write to Vernor's distributors to ask where they can get the ice cream.) Another dairy near Detroit, Risdon's, produced a short-lived ice cream bar in the 1970s with a Vernor's-flavored coating.

In July 1973 a new Vernor's research and development concept, the first of a hoped-for chain of Big Scoop Ice Cream Shops, opened in suburban Warren, Michigan, after much effort and expense. The company heavily promoted the store "Where Ice Cream is More Fun!" to challenge Baskin-Robbins, the leader in the field. A company press release likened the decor to "a scene out of Willie Wonka's Chocolate Factory," and a colorful interior mural showed the famous Vernor's gnomes making Big Scoop concoctions. The new ice cream shop also featured a "special 'Do Your Own Thing' sundae bar for creative ice cream lovers," as well as Boston coolers, cream ales, floats, cones, banana splits, and shakes. Thirty flavors of ice cream were available. Cones came in kid-size Gnome Cones or Big Scoop Cones for heftier appetites, and certificates of membership in the Gnome Glutton Club were awarded to those who finished off a mountainous dessert known as the Super Scooper.

Detroit graphic artist Ron Bialecki

Concept drawing for the Vernor's

designed the interior of the store and the logos for a whimsical effect. The business plan called for two hundred stores owned by the company and by franchisees around the country, but the parent company soon lost confidence in the concept and killed it. The first and last Big Scoop closed in less than a year—the first, but not the last, product failure overseen by supposedly expert corporate leadership. The company seemed to have lost focus once the family gave up control, but corporate control grew stronger and more remote. In 1979, United Brands bought American Consumer Products. A Chiquita Banana and meatpacking conglomerate based in New York with annual sales of over $3.5 billion, United Brands also sold Morell meat products and distributed root beer. United Brands was itself a subsidiary of American Financial Corporation, a gigantic holding company. Around this time the cost of cane and beet sugar

Big Scoop Ice Cream Shop

The gnome, updated for the Big Scoop Shop

doubled, forcing soft-drink producers to use corn sweeteners, which cost half as much. As national concern over environmental problems grew, bottle bills also drove costs up in several states, especially Michigan, where new legislation required deposits on bottles as well as cans. In Michigan the cans could not even be crushed before return. The cost of handling and storing containers soared as companies tried to comply.

United Brands closed the Vernor's bottling plant on Woodward

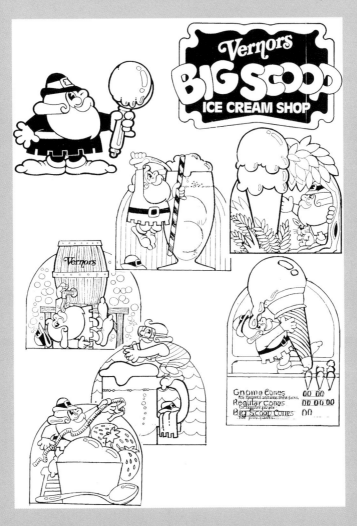

Avenue in 1985, moving manufacture of Detroit's Drink away
from the city, eliminating three hundred jobs, and striking another
blow to the city's morale and tax base as the flight to the suburbs
continued to gain momentum. Vernor's joined a long line of companies fleeing the inner city, including Hudson's, Sears, Federal's,
Crowley's, Sander's, Hughes and Hatcher, Stroh's, Himelhoch's, and
Saks Fifth Avenue.[31] Even the automobile companies were shrink-

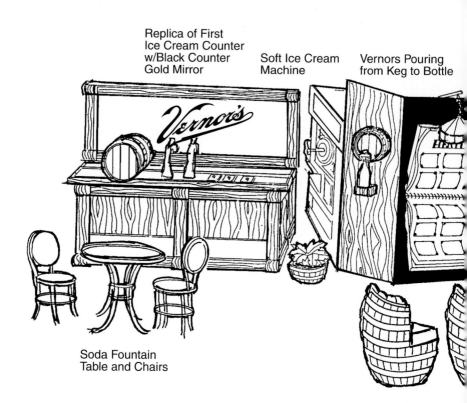

Replica of First
Ice Cream Counter
w/Black Counter
Gold Mirror

Soft Ice Cream
Machine

Vernors Pouring
from Keg to Bottle

Soda Fountain
Table and Chairs

ing from downtown Detroit locations; today only one automobile
plant survives within the Detroit city limits.

Vernor's president at the time, Tom Silinski, announced a plan
to seek a federal grant of $3 million to help construct a new
$13.5 million plant in an area of Detroit known as the Eastern
Market.[32] Mayor Coleman Young helped out with an Urban
Development Action Grant for about one-third the cost of the
proposed 36,000-square-foot plant. The company had recently
started to overcome credit problems caused by its large pension-
fund liabilities and was showing a profit again.[33] The suburbs of
Taylor and Westland also vied for the new plant.

However, the plan to build a new Vernor's plant in the Eastern
Market location never materialized. Chicago developers bought

Frosted Plexiglass
on Ends of Barrels Showing
Rear-Projected Slides and Film

Vernors Pouring
from Bottle to Glass

the Woodward Avenue plant for $25,000, planning a shopping center, but then abandoned the idea a few years later and sold the property to Wayne State University.[34] The old Vernor's site at 4501 Woodward is now a parking lot for Wayne State University.

With its glorious factory gone and renewed hopes for business in Detroit stifled, Vernor's turned over bottling operations altogether to independent franchise bottlers. Pepsi bottlers in Detroit and surrounding areas took over the bottling of Vernor's. Extract production continued at the Taylor plant, and the headquarters were moved to Southfield, a northwest suburb of Detroit.

Further changes occurred in October 1987 when A&W Brands acquired the company for $11 million in cash and A&W shares.[35] In 1986 A&W Brands had sales of almost $60 million, which climbed to $100 million in 1988 after the Vernor's acquisition.[36] The Dallas investment company Hicks & Haas, the largest stockholder of A&W Brands, led the buyout. They were well known for acquiring suffering soft-drink companies, controlling about 15 percent of the U.S. soft-drink market at the time.[37] Vernor's had distribution in twenty-two states, but an A&W executive said, "My feeling is that it will be difficult at best to get a national brand out of this product because it is not ... mainstream...."[38] (A later corporate owner of Vernor's would concur by describing the brand as "only regional" and contrasting it with such "mainstream" brands as A&W Root Beer and Sunkist Orange Soda.)

A&W acquired a unique niche product with a loyal customer following and additional bottlers and distribution points. Two years earlier Vernor's had planned to go national with a million dollar ad campaign. Now a well-funded and financially sound company with the power to expand Vernor's customer base was in control.

In April 1987, Vernor's launched Vernor's California Natural on

I read the letters about Boston coolers (Vernor's and ice cream), and it reminded me of a time when we first moved out here to the Boston area. I went up to the ice cream stand and said I'd have a Boston cooler, figuring that this would definitely be the area to get one. They looked at me like I sprouted an extra head and asked "What's a Boston cooler?" I said you make it with Vernor's and ice cream. They said, "What's Vernor's?" I said it is the best ginger ale. They said they had ginger ale, but still didn't know what a Boston cooler was. I said, "you add ice cream to ginger ale and blend" (that's the way we made them instead of as a float). They said, "Oh, you want a frappe." So I asked what a frappe was, and they said ice cream blended with soda (in this case pale, dry ginger ale, and not Vernor's). So I said,

"OK then,
I'll just have an
ice cream cone." And
they said, "Jimmies?" So I
said "What's Jimmies?" They
said, "Chocolate sprinkles." I
said, "No thanks," and they said,
"Stago?" Again with my extra-head-
ed look, they said, "Would you like to
eat it here? Is this-to-go?" So now I
order ginger ale frappes stago on occa-
sion, but they still don't taste as good as
with Vernor's, like
they do when I
visit the folks
in the Detroit
area.
—Bob
Buchheister

the West Coast. This fruit-flavored soft-drink line, which was not included in the A&W acquisition, included lemon-lime, apple-cranberry, mandarin-lime, mandarin-orange, grapefruit, and low-calorie versions of these flavors. California Natural was a natural disaster, with the product continuing to ferment as it sat unsold on the shelf so that disagreeable flavors developed and some bottles exploded.[39] As with Big Scoop Ice Cream, corporate management could not seem to replicate the high standards and customer appeal the company had enjoyed for so long as a family business.

On October 13, 1993, Cadbury Schweppes, PLC completed a buyout of A&W Brands for U.S.$334 million thereby acquiring the Vernor's brand. By 1994 Cadbury Schweppes had acquired Dr Pepper/Seven-Up and the Vernor's brand came under the control of Dr Pepper/Seven-Up headquarters in Plano, Texas.

Today, Vernor's sales have continued to grow slowly. Vernor's is currently offered in only fifteen states, mainly throughout the Midwest, Florida, and California, its traditional strong mar-

The California Naturals line—like a fault, a disaster waiting to happen

kets. It can also be purchased online from a number of sources. The Detroit area remains its strongest market, where only Pepsi and Coke outsell it. In the rest of the country, however, Vernor's is a minor player with a market share barely one-tenth of 1 percent, sometimes taking a year to sell what Coke sells in three days.[40] Whether Vernor's could have survived the soft-drink market's fierce competition without corporate assimilation is doubtful. By 1998, former rivals Canada Dry and Vernor's ginger ales belonged to the same corporation. The weak have vanished and the strong have adapted. Persisting through corporate takeovers, bad management decisions, and labor strife, Vernor's maintains its loyal following with a strength of market grip that must originate in those barrels of secret flavorings where its delicious difference develops.

Finessing the Fizz

Creating Vernor's Identity

Broad as a Barn

Vernor's Murals in Michigan

Hand-painted advertising signs on the sides of barns, stores, and factories used to be a common sight all across the U.S. Vernor's used this popular advertising method of the era as well with huge painted signs that often included the popular gnome character. One hand-painted sign was uncovered during a construction project in East Lansing, Michigan, across the street from Michigan State University. Ray Myers, the 73-year-old man who had painted the sign in 1955, came forward to have his

Painter of Vernor's Sign Knew It Would Be Found

By Jesse De La Cruz

EAST LANSING—Almost 50 years ago, Ray Myers went out on a routine assignment to paint a Vernor's ginger ale advertisement on the corner of M.A.C. and Grand River avenues.

Today, that handiwork has new life as a local attraction and piece of nostalgia of a forgotten era.

For Myers, 73, it is also a vivid image of the beginnings of his sign-painting career. He considers it one of his best signs, although it was covered only a few months after he painted it in 1955.

The sign re-emerged in February, when the Byrnes Building that protected it was razed to make way for the $30 million City Center development.

"It was like digging up old bones," said Myers, a lifelong Lansing resident.

"We've even said if they ever tear the building down, there it will be—and it was."

Some people want to preserve the sign, perhaps through an acrylic or glass window of the new building. If that doesn't happen, it's likely to be covered by the end of June.

It took a few days for Myers to paint the sign, from putting the primer on to filling the charcoal powder outline that would later be colored.

"I painted Vernor's walls all around Lansing," said Myers, who worked for the Dyer Sign Company at the time. "The only difference was on this one we put a little Sparty hat on [the gnome]."

The Vernor's sign has become a topic of many conversations at the Curious Book Shop, which is in the building the sign is on.

Owner Ray Walsh wants to make a postcard from a picture of the sign that was dropped off at his store.

"It's a vanished East Lansing," Walsh said. "It's an asset of East Lansing that's going to be hidden."

The 1955 sign was not unusual for its time. Hand-painted advertisements decorated many buildings in the Lansing area and nationwide.

It's the nostalgia of the Vernor's sign that makes it important to local people, said Janice Bukovac, assistant professor in the advertising department at Michigan State University.

"I think for a lot of people that is old East Lansing," she said. "That in and of itself is a very important value of the community and people from this area."

Bukovac said the old-fashioned style of advertising also has become popular as an art form.

In Flint, the Greater Flint Arts Council has raised money several times over the past 30 years to save a three-story Vernor's advertisement on its office downtown.

The mural, painted in 1932, features the Vernor's gnomes storing soda syrup in oak barrels and taking them to their castle.

"It has that fairyland appeal to the young people," said Greg Fiedler, the council's executive director. "It's always been a community attraction."

Sign of the times: Ray Myers stands in front of a Vernor's advertisement he painted at the corner of M. A. C. and Grand River avenues about 50 years ago. His work was recently uncovered when a building was razed.

Photo: Chris Holmes/Lansing State Journal

picture taken in front of the sign when it was uncovered, saying that he always knew it would be found some day. Because of the sign's campus location, the gnome was painted wearing a "Sparty" helmet, showing his support for the Michigan State Spartans. Myers painted Vernor's signs on buildings all over the greater Lansing area.

Evolution of bottle design up to the gnome's last days

University of Michigan students also had a Vernor's mural to encourage their consumption of Vernor's Ginger Ale. The faded sign covers one whole side of a building that can easily be seen by students driving back to campus. Today the building houses a small business selling vintage guitars, with the vintage advertising sign providing an additional nostalgic note.

A three-story painted sign in Flint, Michigan, became such a beloved landmark that citizens rallied to save it several times. The three-story mural from 1932 shows several Vernor's gnomes at work, filling their oak barrels and carrying them back to their castle. The painted mural is located on the side of a building housing the offices of the greater Flint Arts Council, which led the effort to save the advertising mural.

UP IN MICHIGAN

Back in the 1950s and 1960s, soft drink companies provided free illuminated signs for stores and small restaurants. Most were Coke or Pepsi signs, but in Michigan, Vernors competed with the big boys. The Vernors sign in this photograph marked the Hersey General Store for decades.

Though it recently went out of business, the general store was the center of commerce in Hersey for a good share of the 20th century. I remember going into the store in the 1960s and seeing groceries, overalls, lanterns, axes, socks, fishing tackle, and sundry other supplies. The era of the general store ended as chain stores in nearby towns offered lower prices and more selection.

Brewed in Detroit, Vernors has been a favorite soft drink in Michigan for decades. With its strong ginger flavor and aggressive carbonation (think bubbles in the nose when you drink a glass of it!), it is a lively alternative to more insipid pop. Vernors is traditionally aged in oak barrels for four years; thirty years ago the village of Hersey, Michigan, the location of this photograph, was a storage center for these oak containers. Little buildings scattered on the edges of town were stuffed to the rafters with oak barrels.

—Lee Rentz

Hersey General Store

Copyright © 2000 by Lee Rentz

Booklets That Tell the Story of

THE story of Vernor's Ginger Ale is dramatically told in a series of six booklets.

They were written expressly for employees of the Vernor Company to give them an idea as to the historical background of the Company, an understanding of its policies and a general picture of its planned expansion.

Size 3½ by 5 inches—a handy pocket size. The covers are attractively printed in color, the pages are profusely illustrated and the text is written in a fast-moving interesting style.

The reproductions below show the range of subjects. There are six booklets to the set. Order by sets.

No. 43-1
It's a Real Story
.05 ea.

No. 43-2
The Secret of Vernor's Goodness
.08 ea.

No. 43-3
Our Share in Victory
.06 ea.

No. 43-4
The Home of Vernor's Gnome
.06 ea.

No. 43-5
Our Future With Vernor's
.06 ea.

No. 43-6
Design for Distribution
.06 ea.

Worker pride and customer satisfaction

U-0101 and U-0102

U-0101

This beautiful display, in 4-color lithography, speaks of the highest in quality point-of-purchase and will be well received by dealers. It admirably points out the advertising theme "Vernors Goes With Everything". Display Card is mounted on stout cardboard with double-wing easel, and designed to be used where permanence of display is required.

U-0102

The soft sheet poster is for general wide coverage at a minimum cost.

Chargeable against your Advertising Account

U-0101 DISPLAY CARD		U-0102 POSTER	
Size:	20'' x 16'' Mounted	Size:	20'' x 16'' Unmounted
Packing:	25 Per Carton	Packing:	50 Per Carton
Weight:	18 lbs. Per Carton	Weight:	5 lbs. Per Carton
Price:	$.49 Each Subject to Change	Price:	$.34 Each Subject to Change
F.O.B.	Detroit, Mich.	F.O.B.	Detroit, Mich.

Order from: Vernors Inc., 4501 Woodward Ave., Detroit, Mich. 48201

U-0101 & U-0102 POWELL ASSOCIATES 500 4-66 LITHO IN U.S.A.

Ad copy and illustrations were available to franchisees.

CLOCKS: Large 20"

20" round illuminated clock with all metal case . . . soft "satin brass" finished rim . . . glass dial screened in permanent brilliant enamels — red, green and yellow . . . illuminated by four 25-Watt incandescent bulbs . . . black minute and hour hands — red sweep second hand to attract attention . . . four covers on back for ease in replacement of bulbs . . . bottom set rod for changing time . . . convex glass completely protects dial and hands . . . 8 foot cord with plug.

Chargeable against your Advertising Account.

J-8040 - 20" ROUND CLOCK

Packing:	One per Carton
Weight:	5 lbs. per Carton
Price:	▬▬▬▬▬ 14.78 Each - Subject to Change
F.O.B.	Detroit, Michigan

Order from: Vernors Inc., 4501 Woodward, Detroit, Mich. 48201

1965

Drink

Vernors

deliciously different

First and second logos. In the first design *(left)*,
the letters *V G A* stand for Vernor's Ginger Ale.

In 1986 the words *Ginger Ale* disappeared from Vernor's containers, packaging, and advertising copy. The managers at A&W decided that ginger ale did not do justice to Vernor's unique flavor and striking difference from their other ginger ale brands, Schweppes and Canada Dry. Members of a test group unfamiliar with Vernor's were at a loss to describe the taste until prompted with the hint "ginger, vanilla, and natural spices." Today's marketing wisdom classifies Vernor's as a ginger soda with a "Barrel Aged, Bold Taste."

For those out-of-state collectors, I have seen "collector" edition glass Vernor's bottles in some gas stations in mid-Michigan with the old Santa Claus–like man on them. I was told by someone who no longer lives near Michigan that Vernor's in bottles always tasted [better] than from cans. I agree. Also, about Vernor's floats: it used to be a treat on Sunday nights for us to have a bowl of ice cream. My favorite was vanilla with Vernor's poured over it. I didn't notice the foam so much, but rather, how it made the outside of the ice cream crusty. That's what I really liked—skim the crust off in a spoon and eat that first.

—Jim Shirey

Take Home a Gnome

Collecting Vintage Vernor's Items

The Gnomemobile

An active collector's market exists for vintage items sporting the Vernor's script logo or the image of the beloved gnome. A wide variety of vintage Vernor's items can be found in antique shops and on Internet sales sites such as eBay. Some people collect anything and everything relating to Vernor's; others specialize in a particular item (vintage glass bottles or porcelain signs). Recent Vernor's items listed for sale on eBay

87

Detail from a holiday greeting card, 1980s

included vintage model cars, trucks, and railroad cars; a coin bank shaped like a Vernor's can; a large green cooler with the Vernor's script logo; wood shipping cartons; bottle openers; and even a paper soda jerk hat from 1967. Some of the most popular collectibles are vintage tin and porcelain advertising signs and large wall clocks, especially if the winking gnome is included. A porcelain advertising sign from the 1950s sold on eBay in January 2003 for $304 and a vintage wall clock for $202.50. A vintage outdoor display thermometer recently offered on eBay revealed some clever marketing efforts to

When Greg and I met
force, he would go on and on about
called Vernor's. He couldn't wait to introduce
He talked about it in his sleep (better that than some
brothers mailed him a six-pack, and he gently chilled it and
wildlife. The big moment came: the uncorking, the sipping, the
It made me sneeze. Vernor's makes everyone sneeze the first time
carbonation will impress you first. This is not a ginger ale for the wimpy!

1960s gnome

1970s gnome

encourage drinking Vernor's both heated and
ice cold. The center of the round thermometer
urges: "Drink Vernor's Ginger Ale in any weather,"
and around the perimeter of the thermometer
is this catchy advice: "Serve hot in cold weather.
Serve cold in hot weather." Even a single vintage
glass Vernor's bottle can find a new home with a collector who wants to remember how it was to gulp down
that bubbly gold Vernor's on a muggy Michigan night
forty or fifty years ago.

A gnome doll sold
at promotions and
in stores and given
away at hospitals and
various events

and were in the air
this fantastic soda from Michigan
me to Vernor's. He dreamed about Vernor's.
former girl friend I suppose). Finally one of his
cooed to it like some endangered species of arctic
savoring, the settling back for smiling and reminiscing.
they try it. . . . Either the strong ginger flavor or the
This has a backbone and a half.   *—The Michie Family*

The Vernor's gnome appeared in the early 1900s, an invention of James Vernor II that was first drawn by the artist Noble Fellows. The gnome almost always appeared along with the Vernor's oaken barrel, a logical device since gnomes were reputed to guard treasure, in this case the mellowing secret-flavor elixir. The gnome usually winks knowingly, as if delighting in the secret of Vernor's delicious difference that he shares with those who love the bubbly beverage.

Sometime in 1968, Vernor's advertising artist Ron Bialecki decided to grow a beard. The company had just decided to soften the gnome's features and make him look friendlier. Vernor's employees, noticing that Bialecki resembled the mythical guardian of the flavor, nicknamed him "the Gnome." Company executives saw the marketing potential of a real, live gnome, and in a few years an office joke became a valuable advertising asset. Bialecki donned a costume made by his wife, Jean, and modified a new, custom,

Vernor's-yellow AMC Pacer to be a rolling ginger-ale keg and promotional juggernaut. In this Gnomemobile he memorably made the rounds of Detroit public events, autographing hundreds of thousands of photographs like the one shown here. The live gnome kept a busy and varied schedule, from such grand events as the state fair and Cobo Hall galas to impromptu, game-stopping ginger-ale giveaways at sandlot baseball games. He delighted children at hospitals, picnics, and youth clubs and became the unofficial mascot of James Vernor Elementary School, where the children were proud of their special association with the avuncular yet otherworldly creature. He wore a custom-built watch with a gnome face, its right eye blinking once per second.

The gnome logged many exhausting hours of entertaining children and quenching thirsts with ginger-ale giveaways, both big-time and backyard, until the company dropped the gnome in the 1980s, wishing to simplify the packaging look. The Vernor's gnome still survives in many happy childhood memories.

Concept for a later and more elaborate Gnomemobile that featured
a platform stage on top, where a gnome-costumed ventriloquist
(Bill Hart) and his dummy gnome conversed while pixie-attired
"gnomettes" handed out ginger ale and promotional items.
The contest challenged contestants to "gname the gnome";
the winning entry was *Jerome.*

*One of my fondest memories is of the summer holidays in
our backyard. Soft drinks were a rare treat, but every
Memorial Day, 4th, and Labor Day, my dad would break
out the aluminum Coleman ice chest, plunk it under the
big maple tree in our backyard, and fill it with Vernor's
Ginger Ale or the different sodas you could buy at Whistle
Pop Stop beside Angie's Pizza. . . . All of us neighborhood kids
would play hard all day, and drink ourselves silly from
that old cooler. What a treat!*
—Bob Reed

A non-street-legal miniature Gnomemobile built
on a go-cart chassis by gnome performer
and designer Ron Bialecki

Vernor's is great with scotch!! Why is it so hard
to find even before having a drink? It is by far one
of the best ginger ales around. I think A&W
distributes it, but they're doing a lousy job of it.
Pepsi should distribute it and maybe we can all get a
look at Britney Spears guzzling some of that
tasty Vernor's down the old hatch.
I guess that would be young hatch
but you can still get the visual.
—Big Daddy

deliciously different

FLAVOR
MELLOWED IN WOOD
4 YEARS

Vernors

SHAKE UP
your drinkin'

Vernors

Sticker given away at public events promoting the U-64 unlimited hydroplane boat sponsored by the company during Detroit's boat-racing heyday. The thirteen-foot *Miss Vernor*, a former *Miss Budweiser*, competed in the Gar Wood Trophy races, now known as the Gold Cup series.

TIPS THE SCALE IN YOUR FAVOR

1 CALORIE

New artificially sweetened Vernors 1 Calorie contains only one calorie per six ounces. Still gives you the same deliciously different flavor of regular Vernors. The only thing taken out are the calories.

VA-VA-VOOM

Circa 1962

8 OZ. CARTON

VA-VA-VOOM
DELICIOUSLY DIFFERENT

8 OZ., 12 OZ. OR 16 OZ. BOTTLE

DELICIOUSLY DIFFERENT

2 columns x 5 inches

Mat Number...................... S-0007
Price Per Mat...................... $00.40

12 OZ. CAN

1 column x 3 inches

Mat Number...................... S-0008
Price Per Mat...................... $00.15

Can't buy Vernor's around my
part of SE Minnesota. Some grocers
did carry it for a couple years in their specialty
pop sections for a very premium price. Over the two
plus decades, I've been here, I've managed to bring back
some amount of Vernor's nearly each trip to Michigan. Almost
everyone here who I have ever introduced to Vernor's has loved it.
Only one did not; he hated it. I try not to introduce too many to it
as I learned just how quickly they can consume my limited supply.
But I don't know any other way to explain it to people than to
give them a taste. I've tried to say it is a brand of ginger ale.
But it is not very close in taste to anything else on the
market called ginger ale. To me it is ginger ale and
all other brands are a far distant second.
——Ray Hicks

Deliciously Different

Drinks

&

Dishes

Recipes Using Vernor's

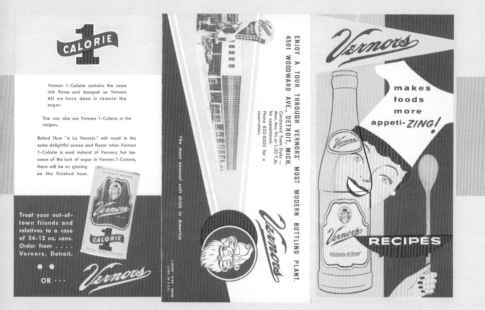

CALORIE 1

Vernors 1-Calorie contains the same rich flavor and bouquet as Vernors. All we have done is remove the sugar.

You can also use Vernors 1-Calorie in the recipes.

Baked Ham "A La Vernors" will result in the same delightful aroma and flavor when Vernors 1-Calorie is used instead of Vernors; but because of the lack of sugar in Vernors 1-Calorie, there will be no glazing on the finished ham.

Treat your out-of-town friends and relatives to a case of 24-12 oz. cans. Order from .... Vernors, Detroit.

OR ...

Vernors

ENJOY A TOUR THROUGH VERNORS' MOST MODERN BOTTLING PLANT. 4501 WOODWARD AVE., DETROIT, MICH.

Conducted from Daily — Mon. thru Fri. at 1.30 P.M., by appointment. Phone 833-8500 for a reservation.

The most unusual soft drink in America

Vernors

Vernors

makes foods more appeti-*ZING!*

Vernors

Vernors
deliciously different

RECIPES

DELICIOUSLY · · DIFFERENT · · RECIPES

 VERNORS **HOT** with LEMON

The rich tang and subtle flavor of cold VERNORS is most inviting when the beverage is served at a temperature not higher than forty degrees. You'll find thoroughly chilled VERNORS satisfying whenever you're thirsty.

◀ RECIPES ▶

For Children Who Are Tired of Milk

VERNORS mixed with equal portions of milk is a drink children find irresistible. Easy to prepare, it's a healthful, rich beverage with a stimulating zest and sparkle. Children ask for more. Serve it often and give the youngsters the wholesome benefits of good milk and pure VERNORS.

VERNOR'S Cream Ale

Put one and one-half ounces (3 tbsp.) of chilled Sweet Cream in each glass and fill with ice cold VERNORS. (For flavor-variety 1½ oz. of any syrup flavoring may be added.) Quick and easy to make, Cream Ale made with VERNORS is an inviting drink anytime.

VERNOR'S Ice Cream Soda

Here's another invigorating treat for both children and grown-ups: Put one or two tablespoonfuls of vanilla ice cream in a tall glass and fill the glass with sparkling, bubbling VERNORS.

VERNOR'S Float

Fill tall beverage glasses two-thirds full of VERNORS and add a scoop of Pineapple Sherbet. Garnish with sprigs of Mint.

VERNOR'S Frappé (5 servings)

1 24-oz. bottle VERNORS
1 pt. Ice Cream (any flavor)

Place Ice Cream in chilled dish or in dish surrounded by ice cubes. Pour ice cold VERNORS slowly over Ice Cream, stirring until you have a smooth mixture with no remaining ice cream lumps. Garnish each glass with Cherry, or if Chocolate Ice Cream is used, bits of Marshmallow are attractive.

VERNOR'S Fruit Punch

1 12-oz. can pineapple juice
1 12-oz. can grape juice
1 quart VERNORS

Serve at once with crushed ice.

YOUR OWN Chilled Beverage Creations . . .

will be brightened by using VERNORS instead of water. VERNORS adds sparkle and scintillating flavor to any fruit drink, gelatin or frozen recipe. Be sure to have VERNORS thoroughly chilled and add it as late as possible, pouring slowly to preserve carbonation.

◀ DINNER ▶

VERNOR'S Frozen Fruit Cocktail (6 servings)

½ cup crushed pineapple
2 cups orange pulp
¾ cup grapefruit pulp
1½ cups powdered sugar
1 cup VERNORS (throughly chilled)

Add the sugar to the fruits and stir gently until sugar is dissolved, then add the VERNORS. Pour into small molds or into freezing tray of electric refrigerator. Makes a delicious salad or appetizer.

Baked Ham a la VERNORS

Boil ham until tender, discarding water. Remove skin and excess fat. Rub liberally with brown sugar and stick cloves into surface. Place in baking utensil, adding contents of one or two bottles of VERNORS — according to size of ham — sufficient to baste generously. Bake in slow oven until ham is heated through. Baste every fifteen minutes. This ham is delightful for cold plate or served as it comes from the oven. VERNORS, used in basting, is a simple way to bring to meats a new, delightful aroma and flavor.

VERNOR'S Gelatine Dessert

Use VERNORS instead of water in any regular gelatine or jello recipe to give your desserts unusual appeal. The original flavor of VERNORS is emphasized when used with plain gelatine. Also very good with lemon jello. Fruits may be added to make a variety of "deliciously different" desserts.

Peppermint Ale Fizz

1 quart VERNORS
½ lb. peppermint stick candy
2 cups whipping cream

Put the candy through a food chopper or roll with rolling pin. Whip cream to custard-like consistency and fold in candy crumbs, then place in freezing tray of refrigerator to freeze. To serve: Place serving of frozen peppermint cream in tall frosted glass and fill with chilled VERNORS. Stir slightly with spoon to make it fizz and serve with spoon and straw.

Doctors and dieticians recommend VERNORS. Vernors is pure and wholesome. It is the healthful beverage that has won the preference of children and grown-ups alike.

When you are cold.....

DRINK

Served **HOT** (WITH LEMON)

Here's a treat as original and surprising as the famous VERNOR'S flavor itself. Heat VERNOR'S to the boiling point in a glass or metal container, then pour over a small piece of lemon. It's especially welcome on a cold day after outdoor activity.

HEALTHFUL · WARMING · STIMULATING

Vernor's striking flavor

makes it, as one sales manual put it, "such a complete refreshment in itself that it seems to be 'gilding the lily' to suggest its use in concocting mixed drinks and other delicacies." However, as a way to increase sales the company developed recipe leaflets and supplied them to retailers for years. Customers contributed hundreds of recipes to Vernor's cuisine, many of which made it into later leaflets such as the "Vernors Lovers Recipe Book." (All recipes reproduced here require genuine Vernor's Ginger Ale for best results.)

We asked you to use your imagination, and you did! With Vernors recipes for scrumptious desserts, exotic casseroles, zesty beverages and marvelous meat dishes. We couldn't have done it without you. To the Vernors lovers of America, we say...enjoy!

Contents

GINGER ALE SALAD

3-ounce package lime gelatin
3-ounce package lemon gelatin
2 cups Vernors, heated to boiling

20-ounce can crushed pineapple
1 cup diced celery
Small bottle maraschino cherries
1/2 cup chopped nuts

Dissolve gelatin in hot Vernors and let cool. Stir in pineapple with juice, celery, drained cherries and nuts. Turn into mold and chill until firm.

Dorothy M. Senkpiel, Saginaw, Mich.

MOUNTAIN TOP GREEN SALAD

6-ounce package lime gelatin
2 cups hot water
1 can Vernors
1 cup finely ground nuts

1 pound can crushed pineapple in own juice
1 sliced banana
9-ounce package topping mix
Maraschino cherries

Dissolve gelatin in hot water. Cool and add Vernors, then chill until syrupy. Add nuts, pineapple and banana. Chill until almost firm. Prepare topping and mix into gelatin. Turn into mold and decorate with cherries. Cover with plastic wrap and chill in refrigerator.

Mrs. Mildred Campbell, Flat Rock, Mich.

LEMON-PEAR MOLD

3-ounce package lemon gelatin
1/2 cup boiling water
1-1/2 cups Vernors

6 canned pear halves
4 tablespoons toasted almond halves
1 tablespoon finely cut candied ginger

Dissolve gelatin in boiling water. Stir in Vernors, then pour about 1 cup of mixture in flat pan or mold and chill until slightly thick. Arrange pear halves on gelatin, sprinkle with almonds and ginger and pour in remaining gelatin. Chill until firm, then cut so each serving has a pear. Place on lettuce and serve with salad dressing.

Eleanor M. Brewer, New Haven, Mich.

2

CHEESE-FRUIT MOLD

3-ounce package lemon gelatin
2 cups Vernors, heated to boiling

8-ounce package cream cheese
16-ounce can fruit cocktail, drained

Dissolve gelatin in hot Vernors. Stir in chunks of cream cheese and mix until blended. Refrigerate until slightly thickened. Fold in fruit cocktail and turn into mold or serving dish. Chill until firm.

Rachel Zack, Wyandotte, Mich.

VERNORS CHEESE MOLD

1 envelope unflavored gelatin
1 small can crushed pineapple

3-ounce package cream cheese
1/4 cup sugar
1 can Vernors

Mix gelatin with 1/2 cup juice drained from pineapple. Heat and stir until dissolved. Beat cream cheese and sugar, gradually adding Vernors until smooth. Stir in gelatin mixture and pineapple, turn into a mold and chill about two hours. Serve with pork, ham or turkey.

Mrs. Hazel Maul, Roseville, Mich.

APPLE GINGER ALE SALAD

2 tablespoons unflavored gelatin
2 tablespoons cold water
1/3 cup boiling water
1 cup Vernors
1/4 cup lemon juice
Dash salt

2 tablespoons sugar
1/3 cup chopped celery
1/3 cup chopped apple
1/3 cup canned crushed pineapple
2 tablespoons chopped candied ginger

Soften gelatin in cold water, stir in boiling water until dissolved. Stir in Vernors, lemon juice, salt and sugar and chill until it starts to thicken. Fold in celery, apple, pineapple and ginger. Chill until firm and serve with a tart dressing.

Mrs. Karl E. Brown, Detroit, Mich.

3

LIME-GINGER SALAD

6-ounce package lime
  gelatin
2 cups Vernors, heated
  to boiling
2 cups chilled Vernors

2 cups diced fresh pears
1 cup minced celery
Whipped cream
Minced crystallized
  ginger

Dissolve lime gelatin in hot Vernors. Add remaining
Vernors and chill until partially set. Fold in pears and
celery, turn into 8-inch square pan and chill until
firm. Serve on lettuce and garnish with whipped
cream and minced ginger. Serves 12.

Ms. Loretta J. Michalczak, Hamtramck, Mich.

CRANBERRY-RASPBERRY MOLD

6-ounce package
  raspberry gelatin
1 cup boiling water
1-pound can whole
  cranberry sauce

10-ounce package
  frozen raspberries
1 cup Vernors
1/4 cup lemon juice
2 tablespoons shredded
  orange peel

Dissolve gelatin in boiling water. Add cranberry
sauce and stir until blended. Add raspberries,
Vernors, lemon juice and orange peel. Pour into
lightly oiled two-quart mold and chill until firm.
Serves 8.

Mrs. Jean Volos, Detroit, Mich.

MOLDED GINGER PEAR SALAD

3-ounce package lemon
  gelatin
1 cup boiling water
3/4 cup chilled Vernors

6 pear halves
Lemon juice
Cottage cheese

Dissolve gelatin in water, cool, then stir in Vernors.
Dip pear halves in lemon juice and arrange in ring
mold. Pour gelatin mixture over pears and chill until
firm. Unmold and fill center with cottage cheese.

Mrs. S. Hammes, Trenton, Mich.

4

GINGER ALE MARSHMALLOW SALAD

1 pound marshmallows
2 tablespoons fruit juice
2 cups Vernors
1 cup mayonnaise
1-1/2 cups drained
  crushed pineapple

2 cups chopped canned
  peaches
1/2 cup chopped
  maraschino cherries
1 cup whipping cream,
  whipped

Combine marshmallows and fruit juice in top of
double boiler. Place over hot water and stir constantly until marshmallows are melted. Cool, then
stir in ginger ale, mayonnaise, pineapple, peaches
and cherries and mix well. Fold in whipped cream
and turn into individual molds. Freeze until serving
time. Serve on crisp lettuce with mayonnaise.
Makes about 25 molds.

Mrs. Albert G. Kullberg, Bay City, Mich.

GINGER-PEACHY MELBA PARFAIT PIE

3-ounce package peach
  gelatin
3-ounce package red
  raspberry gelatin
3 cups hot Vernors

1 pint vanilla or peach
  ice cream
1 cup canned peach
  slices, drained
Baked 10-inch pie shell

Dissolve peach and raspberry gelatins in hot Vernors.
Chill until syrupy and thick. Whip until frothy, then
stir in ice cream until melted and well blended. Fold
in peaches which have been cut in bite-sized pieces.
Turn into pie shell and chill until firm. Garnish with
whipped cream and additional peach slices if desired.

Mrs. P. M. Rothwell, Birmingham, Mich.

GINGER BAKED APPLES

Place six peeled and cored apples in shallow pan.
Pour in Vernors to cover bottom of pan. Sprinkle
apples with cinnamon and pour more Vernors into
apple centers. Bake at 375 degrees about 45 minutes.

Pat Housner, Brighton, Mich.

5

FRUIT COMPOTE

1 apple, peeled and
  cubed
1 pear, peeled and
  cubed
1 banana, sliced

1 orange, cut in small
  pieces
1 teaspoon lemon juice
Chilled Vernors

Combine prepared fruit and lemon juice in bowl.
Pour in enough Vernors to cover fruit. Cover and
refrigerate one hour before serving. Serves two.

Mary Kulikous, Detroit, Mich.

VERNORS GINGER ALE PIE

2 cups Vernors
1/2 cup brown sugar
1/3 cup flour
1/8 teaspoon salt

3 egg yolks
2 tablespoons butter or
  margarine
Baked 9-inch pie shell

Heat Vernors to scalding. Blend sugar, flour and salt.
Add to hot mixture and beat until smooth. Beat egg
yolks and stir into mixture. Mix well and cook and stir

6

until thickened. Stir in butter. Pour into baked pie
shell and top with meringue made from egg whites.

Mrs. Esther H. Taylor, Inkster, Mich.

FESTIVE CAKE

1 cup Vernors
1 cup orange juice
1 pound marshmallows
1 pint whipping cream,
  whipped

Baked angel food cake
Shredded coconut
Chopped nuts
Maraschino cherries

In top of double boiler combine Vernors, orange
juice and marshmallows. Place over hot water and
stir until marshmallows are dissolved. Chill until
thickened, then combine with whipped cream. Break
cake into small pieces. Place in 9 x 12 x 3-inch pan.
Cover with cream mixture so all cake is covered.
Sprinkle with coconut, nuts and cherries. Refrigerate several hours.

Reva DeBruyne, Ann Arbor, Mich.

Recipes Using Vernor's 103

VERNORS-CRANBERRY PUNCH

In large punch bowl mix four cups cranberry juice cocktail, four cups pineapple-grapefruit juice and one and one-half cups sugar. Stir until sugar is dissolved. Stir in two quarts chilled Vernors ginger ale and chill thoroughly.

Mary Ellen Bihn, Toledo, Ohio

FRUIT PUNCH

4 cans frozen orange juice concentrate
Juice of 6 lemons
1 cup sugar
2 cups cold water

1 large can pineapple juice
1 can pineapple chunks
1 small bottle cherries
2 quarts chilled Vernors

In punch bowl mix orange juice concentrate, lemon juice, sugar and water. Add pineapple juice, pineapple chunks and cherries with juice. Add ice block and stir in Vernors.

Mrs. Alfred Weiner, Oak Park, Mich.

VERNORS MINT JULEP

1 bunch fresh mint
1 cup lemon juice
1 cup sugar

1/2 cup water
3 pints chilled Vernors

Mix mint leaves, lemon juice, sugar and water. Let stand 30 minutes. Pour over large ice block in punch bowl, then stir in three pints chilled Vernors. Makes about 20 punch cup servings.

Flo Kosmyna, Toledo, Ohio

SUNSHINE PUNCH

Combine in punch bowl one 6-ounce can frozen orange juice concentrate, one 6-ounce can frozen lemonade concentrate, one 6-ounce can frozen limeade concentrate and one quart cold water. Mix well, then stir in one quart chilled Vernors and ice cubes. Serves 12.

Mrs. Robert H. Briggs, Farmington, Mich.

EASY PUNCH

Combine in punch bowl 6-ounce can frozen orange juice concentrate, 16-ounce can fruit cocktail, 10-ounce package frozen sliced strawberries, one sliced banana and three large bottles chilled Vernors ginger ale. Let stand until strawberries and juice are defrosted, stirring occasionally.

Ann Hooghart, Southfield, Mich.

VERNORS FLOAT

Place two or three scoops vanilla ice cream in tall glasses. Stir in chilled Vernors to fill glasses.

Lynn Anderson, Lansing, Mich.

GINGER TEA

Pour eight ounces hot tea into tall glasses. Stir two ounces Vernors into each glass.

Samuel Cohen, Oak Park, Mich.

MOCK SANGRIA

Mix equal parts of Vernors and grape juice. Serve cold over ice for a refreshing summer drink. Serve hot in mugs with a thin lemon slice for warming winter drink.

Carole Hunt, Dearborn, Mich.

NEW YORKER

In blender or shaker mix six ounces Vernors, two tablespoons chocolate syrup, two tablespoons cream or evaporated milk and crushed ice. Serves one.

Carol White, Woodhaven, Mich.

PASSION-PARTY PUNCH

In punch bowl mix two quarts chilled orange juice one bottle light rum and two quarts chilled Vernors. Garnish with fresh or canned fruit cocktail.

Chuck Incaudo, Troy, Mich.

VERNORS-CHAMPAGNE PUNCH

Empty one large can frozen lemonade concentrate and one large can frozen orange juice concentrate into punch bowl. Stir in three cans cold water and two quarts chilled Vernors. Just before serving gently stir in one bottle chilled champagne. Add ice cubes with maraschino cherries frozen in them or a decorated ice ring. Serves 24.

Mrs. Judy Schmitz, Troy, Mich.

HOT VERNORS WINE PUNCH

Bring two quarts Vernors to boiling over low heat. Remove from heat and pour in one bottle Port wine. Add three or four cinnamon sticks, six whole cloves and thin slices of lemon. Serve hot in mugs.

Sue Strickroot, Sterling Heights, Mich.

WHISKEY SOUR

Place in electric blender one 6-ounce can frozen lemonade concentrate. Using empty can for measuring, add one can whiskey and one can Vernors. Blend at high speed 20 seconds and pour into glasses over crushed ice. Garnish with maraschino cherry and thin orange slice.

Dorothy Popke, Lake City, Mich.

EASY CHICKEN

Combine one quart Vernors and 14-ounce bottle of catsup in large saucepan. Add chicken legs and wings or other chicken parts. Bring slowly to boiling, then reduce heat, cover and simmer about an hour or until chicken is done.

Paula Henson, Allen Park, Mich.

ZESTY MEAT BALLS

2 pounds ground beef	Water
1/4 cup uncooked rice	2 cups Vernors
1 onion, grated	1/2 bottle catsup
1 egg	Cooked rice

Combine beef, uncooked rice, onion and egg. Mix lightly, adding small amount of water. Shape into patties. Combine Vernors and catsup in large pan and bring to boiling. Drop patties into mixture and simmer over low heat one hour. Serve patties with sauce on cooked rice.

Anna Leven, Southfield, Mich.

GINGER POT ROAST

3 to 4 pound pot roast	Dash of salt
4 sliced carrots	Dash of pepper
4 stalks celery, sliced	Dash of garlic powder
1/2 cup sliced onion	3 cups Vernors

Brown meat on both sides and place in roasting pan. Add carrots, celery, onions, salt, pepper, garlic and Vernors. Cover, bake at 325 degrees about three hours. Remove meat to hot platter with vegetables and thicken liquid for gravy.

Mrs. David Lynn, Warren, Mich.

BAKED SAUSAGE

Dissolve one-half to one cup brown sugar in one quart Vernors in shallow roasting pan. Add fresh or smoked Polish or Hungarian sausages. Cover and simmer two to three hours in 300-degree oven. Baste with pan liquids frequently.

Mrs. J. A. Gesh, Wyandotte, Mich.

10

VERNORS SWEET AND ZESTY MEATBALLS

12 ounces Vernors	2 tablespoons chopped parsley
12 ounces catsup	
2 pounds lean ground beef	1 tablespoon oregano
	1 tablespoon garlic salt
1 small onion, chopped	1 cup bread crumbs
	2 eggs

Combine Vernors and catsup in Dutch oven or heavy pan. In large mixing bowl combine beef, onion, parsley, oregano, garlic salt, bread crumbs and eggs. Mix well and form into small 1/2-inch balls. Drop raw meat balls into pot, cover and simmer over low heat one hour. Great for party appetizers. For main dish serve over noodles or rice.

Cindy Kurman, Madison Hts., Mich.

GINGER HAM SLICE

Place fully cooked center cut ham slice (1-inch thick) in shallow baking dish. Pour in one cup Vernors and sprinkle one-fourth cup brown sugar and a dash of ground cloves over meat. Bake at 350 degrees 30 minutes, brushing frequently with liquid. If desired let ham stand in the marinade two hours, then broil over low coals about 15 minutes, brushing with marinade from time to time.

Sheila Cox, Madison Hts., Mich.

BAKED HAM VERNORS

Place five-pound boneless canned ham or any pre-cooked boneless smoked ham fat side down in shallow baking dish. Mix three tablespoons brown sugar with a little Vernors. Pour remainder of small bottle Vernors over ham. With pastry brush cover the ham with the brown sugar mixture. Place aluminum foil over pan and bake at 350 degrees one and one-half hours. Uncover during last 15 minutes.

Mrs. Evelyn Brink, Rockford, Mich.

11

GINGER BAKED BEANS

1 large can pork and beans	1 large tomato, chopped
	1-1/2 cups brown sugar
1 large onion, chopped	1 cup Vernors
1 medium green pepper, chopped	

Mix beans, onion, green pepper and tomato in baking dish. Stir brown sugar into Vernors until dissolved, then pour over beans and bake at 325 degrees about 35 minutes.

Betty Robinson, Lansing, Mich.

VERNORS CHEESE FONDUE

1-1/2 cups Vernors	3 cups (8 ounces) grated Swiss cheese
1 garlic clove, mashed	
	2 tablespoons flour
	Salt and pepper

Heat Vernors and garlic to boiling over medium heat. Blend cheese with flour, then using a fork gradually blend into Vernors, stirring constantly. Season to taste with salt and pepper and place over candle warmer server. Serve with crusty bread cubes. If mixture becomes too thick, stir in more Vernors.

Sara J. Zavos, Dearborn, Mich.

VERNORS BAR-B-Q SAUCE

1 large can tomato sauce	2 tablespoons brown sugar
1 small can tomato paste	2 tablespoons Worcestershire sauce
1-1/4 cups Vernors	2 garlic cloves, mashed or 1/2 teaspoon garlic powder
1 teaspoon salt	
1/2 teaspoon pepper	

Combine tomato sauce and tomato paste. Measure Vernors and let set 30 minutes. Stir into tomato mixture with salt, pepper, sugar, Worcestershire and garlic. Simmer over low heat about an hour or until thickened. Brush on spareribs during last hour of cooking. Great on hamburgers too.

Mrs. K. R. Boonstra, Spring Lake, Mich.

12

Vernor's Frappe

One 24-ounce bottle Vernor's
One pint ice cream (any flavor)

Place ice cream in chilled dish, or in dish surrounded by ice cubes. Pour Vernor's slowly over ice cream, stirring until smooth. Pour into glasses and garnish with cherries (or if chocolate ice cream is used, marshmallows).

Monkey-Spanker

Large jigger bourbon
One 12-ounce can Vernor's

Peppermint Ale Fizz

One quart Vernor's
One-half pound peppermint stick candy
Two cups whipping cream

Finely chop candy in food processor. Whip cream and fold in candy crumbs; freeze. To serve, place a portion of the frozen mixture in tall glasses and fill with Vernor's. Stir lightly with spoon to make fizz and serve with spoon and straw.

Vernor's Cream Ale

Pour three tablespoons of chilled sweet cream into an eight-ounce glass; fill with Vernor's. To vary flavor any syrup flavoring may be added.

Vernor's Slush

2 cups sugar

9 cups water

Bring water and sugar to boil, cool, and add the following:

One 12-ounce can orange juice

One 12-ounce can lemonade mix

One pint of gin or vodka

Mix ingredients and freeze until slushy and scoop into glasses of Vernor's. This mixture can also be frozen into ice cube trays and used as ice cubes. (Credited by Groceries Express to Ruthie Miller of Essexville, Michigan)

Swank Vernor's Punch

One bottle champagne

One bottle sauternes

One bottle club soda

One cup Vernor's

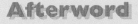

Afterword

America's oldest soft-drink maker, well into its second century
of continuous operation, has seen many changes in the industry,
the city of its origin, and the world. Vernor's remains an icon of
exemplary manufacturing integrity, quality, and business accom-
plishment surviving into an era wherein business in the United
States has come under increasing fire for questionable practices.
James Vernor's vision of producing a quality product and a different taste experience continues to delight even today in a field
of mass-merchandised soft drinks. Although Vernor's occupies a
small niche market and competes with such giants of the industry
as Coke and Pepsi it still enjoys one of the most loyal consumer
bases in the industry. There is nothing fickle about the Vernor's
lover.

From its beginning as a gleam in the eye of a post–Civil War
soldier and pharmacist to its present position as a part of the
huge Cadbury Schweppes conglomerate, Vernor's continues to
enjoy the loyal following that it established soon after its founding
in 1866. Established in a city where fortunes are made and lost
as a matter of course, Vernor's has survived to become the oldest (and one of the best-loved) soft drinks in the United States.
In a city that spawned such giants of industry as Ford Motor
Company, General Motors, Chrysler, Parke-Davis, and U.S. Royal,
this is a remarkable feat and a tribute to the company's founder
and to those that followed. This success is also a tribute to the
loyal Vernor's fanatics who cling lovingly to the green and gold to

this day. The story of Vernor's has but few equals in industrial history, a business success that provided a livelihood to thousands throughout its long history.

Vernor's has contributed millions of dollars to the Detroit economy and later to its shareholders throughout the country. The company also established itself as a leader in efficient and technologically advanced soft-drink manufacturing. In 1941, just before the country entered World War II, Vernor's opened the most modern bottling plant then to exist in the world. Although James Vernor I did not live long enough to see this, having died in 1927, the modern facility represented the culmination of his vision and impact on the soft-drink industry.

Many factors contributed to Vernor's success. Vernor was fortunate that he established his company in a city that would become a hub of industry with the transportation infrastructure that grew to support it. The early economic success of the city and the entrepreneurial spirit of its leaders and its banking industry created a positive atmosphere for growth and an expectation of success. Detroit was a city with a can-do attitude and a willing workforce that immigrated or moved to Detroit to work, and to work hard. The many suppliers and engineers in the city who were capable of building a great manufacturing facility contributed greatly to the company. Detroit was a great cauldron of creativity during the establishment of the auto industry and through the middle-aged years of Vernor's when the company established itself as a leader in the soft-drink industry. Detroit was one of very few places in the country that could have spawned such great industry. Vernor was in the right place at the right time and with the right idea: a deliciously different drink that can't be copied and can't be forgotten.

A CHRONOLOGY **OF EVENTS**
IN THE HISTORY OF VERNOR'S
AND THE SOFT-DRINK INDUSTRY

400 b.c.	Hippocrates writes about the medicinal properties of mineral water.
1520s	Paracelsus, a Swiss physician, writes about the beneficial properties of effervescent mineral waters.
1560	First attempt to create artificial mineral water by Leonhard Thurneysser of Basel, Switzerland.
1608	First blown-glass bottle production starts in Jamestown, Virginia. By the mid-1600s the screw-on cap begins to appear.
1710	Joseph Priestley begins experimenting with "fixed air" and identifies it as carbon dioxide by 1767.
1770	Torbern Bergman of Sweden builds first viable equipment for artificially carbonated water.
1785	Thomas Jefferson and James Madison start to study mineral waters in U.S.
1789	Jacob Schweppe establishes Schweppe and Company in London.
1790	Dr. John Clarke opens the first soda water fountain in the U.S. in New York City. U.S. Patent Office starts to register medicine. The first census of the U.S. is taken, and it is determined that the population of the U.S. is 3,893,874.

1792   Dr. Valentine Seaman of New York describes a process for making artificial mineral water after studying the Saratoga Springs.

1794   Jacob Schweppe opens his first mineral water business in Bristol, England.

1807   Benjamin Silliman, a Yale professor, opens a store dispensing bottled soda water (the first sold in the U.S.).

1809   Joseph Hawkins is awarded first U.S. patent for artificial mineral water.

1810   First U.S. patent is issued for saturating water with carbonic acid gas. The population of the U.S. is now 6,807,786.

1831   Use of carbonate of soda in soft drinks disappears, but generic name remains. Use of flavoring syrups (first used in the late 1700s) starts to spread.

1835   First bottled soda water is produced in U.S.

1836   U.S. Patent Office is destroyed by fire along with all previously filed patents.

1843   James Vernor is born in Albany, New York.

1848   Vernor family moves to Detroit, Michigan.

1850   U.S. Census reports 64 soda water bottling plants, 14 operating in New York City alone.

1851   Ginger ale is introduced in Ireland.

1858   James Vernor takes job at Higby and Stern's (Stearn's).

1860   U.S. Census reports 123 soda water bottling plants. Soda fountains now are as plentiful as saloons. The U.S. population is 31,183,582.

1861   U.S. Civil War starts.

1862   James Vernor joins the Fourth Michigan Cavalry.

1863   James Vernor is captured in battle.

1864 James Vernor is promoted to lieutenant.

1865 Civil War ends. James Vernor returns to Detroit and opens his own drugstore.

1866 Date is later recognized as "official" birth date of Vernor's Ginger Ale. Cantrell & Cochrane of Ireland enter the U.S. market with their ginger ale.

1871 Lemon's Superior Sparkling Ginger Ale becomes the first trademarked soft-drink brand.

1874 Ice cream soda is invented, generally credited to Robert M. Green of Philadelphia, a soda water concessionaire.

Now the woman who would calm my upset stomach with small sips of Vernor's Ginger Ale lives in my home. Now it's my turn. Time moves on.
—Rabbi Steven Kushner

1876 Charles E. Hires begins root beer empire in Philadelphia. Moxie Nerve Food is created in Lowell, Massachusetts (at first is sold as a medicine but later becomes popular as a unique soft drink).

1877 James Vernor II is born.

1879 Saccharin is discovered.

1880 U.S. Census reports 512 bottling plants. U.S. population reaches 49,371,340. Trade magazine *American Bottler* starts publication, followed in 1882 by *National Bottlers' Gazette*. First cola-flavored beverage is created.

1884 Schweppes opens a factory in New York City.

1885 William Painter develops bottle seal, leading to "crown seal" patent issued in 1892. R. S. Lazenby invents Dr Pepper in Waco, Texas.

1886 Dr. John Pemberton, of Atlanta, Georgia, invents

Coca-Cola in his backyard and sells 25 gallons in his first year.

1888   James Vernor is elected Detroit city alderman. Liquid Carbonic Acid Manufacturing Company is established to manufacture liquid gas previously imported from Germany.

1889   U.S. Census reports 1,377 bottling plants. Partial automation of manufacturing process appears.

1892   Crown cork is developed, the first "modern" crimped-on metal cap.

1895   Michael Owens patents semiautomatic glass bottle machine.

1896   James Vernor II enters business with father. Vernor's full-time soft-drink business begins; drugstore closed.

1898   Caleb Bradham, of New Bern, North Carolina, invents drink that will become Pepsi-Cola (see 1902). One year later Coca-Cola appoints its first bottling franchise.

1900   U.S. Census reports 2,763 bottling plants. U.S. population approaches 77,000,000.

1901   The modern era of advertising begins. Coca-Cola spends $100,000 this year, and the first ad for Coca-Cola in bottles appears the following year.

1902   Pepsi-Cola Company is formed in New Bern, North Carolina. Owens fully automates the bottle machine and receives patent in 1904.

1904   Canada Dry starts up in Toronto.

1905   Royal Crown Cola is established in Columbus, Georgia.

1910   U.S. population reaches 92 million. U.S. Census reports 4,916 bottling plants.

1913 Motor trucks start to replace horse-drawn delivery wagons, increasing efficiency greatly.

1914 World War I starts in Europe.

1917 U.S. enters World War I. Federal excise tax is imposed on some soft-drink ingredients to raise money for the war effort.

1918 World War I ends. Riverside Power Plant at foot of Woodward Avenue is purchased and converted to Vernor's bottling plant. National Bottlers Association is formed.

My favorite things are sushi, tea, and Vernor's ginger ale.
—Tasha Kelter

1919 Six-story addition is added to Vernor's Riverside Bottling Plant. American Bottlers of Carbonated Beverages association is formed.

1920 Prohibition starts on January 29. U.S. Census reports 5,000 bottlers in business and 5,194 bottling plants. Automatic cup-vending machines start to appear. Designer bottles are introduced.

1922 Dry ginger ale is introduced to U.S. Canada Dry starts bottling facility in New York State.

1923 Six-packs appear called "Hom-Paks." (They become a standard by 1928.) Glass bottle manufacturers standardize the crown-top bottle.

1925 Number of U.S. soft-drink bottlers peaks, approaching 8,000. Canada Dry opens a plant in New York City.

1927 James Vernor I dies at the age of 84. James Vernor II becomes president of Vernor's Company.

1929 Stock market crashes set off the Great Depression. Number of bottlers reaches historically highest level at about 7,900. Beverage that became 7-Up is introduced as Bib-Label Lithiated Lemon-Lime Soda.

1930   Over 7,500 bottling plants are in operation. U.S. population is 123,076,741.

1931   J. Vernor Davis joins Vernor's Company.

1932   Federal soft-drink tax is reinstated until 1934 to raise revenue to fight Great Depression.

1933   Colored labels on bottles are introduced.

1934   Pepsi introduces "twice as much for a nickel."

1935   Number of bottlers decreases to fewer than 6,100.

1937   Cyclamate is discovered.

1939   Old Siegal building is purchased by Vernor's.

1940   James Vernor IV is born. Over 6,000 bottlers are now in operation. Population reaches 132 million. 12-ounce bottles account for 25 percent of soft-drink production.

1941   United States enters World War II. The "Most Modern Bottling Facility in the World" opens as the company celebrates its 75th anniversary. Wartime shortages and rationing start to affect industry as sugar, cork, metal, and paper become scarce. Bottlers start recycling programs.

1942   Soft drinks are declared an "essential food" by the United States War Board during World War II, thereby insuring a supply for civilians as well as soldiers.

1945   Wartime restrictions are dropped. Sugar remains under controls until 1947.

1948   Sugar Act takes effect to control sugar production and prices. Pepsi is produced in cans for the first time (not a great success; costs were high). First "throwaway, non-refillable" glass bottles introduced.

1951   City of Detroit asks Vernor's to move to old

Convention Center site far up north Woodward
Avenue near Wayne State University.

1952   J. Vernor Davis becomes president of Vernor's
        Company and James Vernor III becomes vice president.
        Kirsch Beverages, of Brooklyn, New York, introduces
        No-Cal, the first diet soft drink.

1954   James Vernor II dies. New plant at 4501 Woodward
        Avenue opens.

1957   James Vernor III dies. Aluminum cans are introduced to
        soft-drink industry. Overall production of soft drinks
        surpasses 1.36 million cases. Number of bottlers down
        to about 5,100 (127 bottlers in Michigan compared
        to 75 in 1900). U.S. population is 171,984,130.

1959   First diet cola is invented.

1962   Can pull-tabs are introduced.

1963   Can vending machines are
        introduced.

1965   Resealable bottle tops are
        invented.

1966   Vernor's sold away from family
        control. American Bottlers of
        Carbonated Beverages changes to
        National Soft Drink Association.

1969   U.S. bans the use of cyclamates. Cadbury
        and Schweppes merge.

1970   Plastic bottles introduced.

1974   The permanent pull-tab for cans is invented. Coke
        and others switch to high-fructose corn syrup (HFCS)
        as sugar prices rise significantly.

> *Vernor's, if
> you don't know what
> it is, can be approximated
> by taking ginger ale, doubling
> the flavor, and adding almost
> enough carbonation to make
> the can explode. It's a
> Detroit thing.*
> —Avi Drissman

1978   Philip Morris acquires the Seven-Up Company.

1981   The first interactive talking vending machine is
        developed.

1982   Dr Pepper buys Canada Dry from
        giant Norton Simon, Inc.

1983   Aspartame/Nutra-Sweet intro-
        duced by the G. D. Searle
        Company and approved by the
        Food and Drug Administration
        (FDA). A year later it will capture 70
        percent of the market. Caffeine-free colas appear.

There isn't much better than a pasty and a Vernor's to go with it. That is classic Michigan cuisine and we are grateful for it.
—Sharon

1984   Federal Trade Commission (FTC) blocks sale of
        Dr Pepper to Coke and Seven-Up to Pepsi on anti-
        competition grounds. Dr Pepper is sold to Forstmann
        Little and Canada Dry to RJR Nabisco.

1985   "New Coke" is introduced, creating one of the greatest
        public-relations blunders ever in the soft-drink business.

1986   Pepsi buys Seven-Up operations located outside the
        U.S. Inside the U.S., Dr Pepper and Seven-Up merge
        and Cadbury Schweppes acquires 30 percent.

1993   Over 384 billion soft-drink containers have been recy-
        cled since 1970. Cadbury Schweppes acquires A&W
        Brands along with the Vernor's brand.

1994   Cadbury Schweppes Beverages acquires Dr Pepper/
        Seven-Up for $1.7 billion and gains a 16 percent share
        of the U.S. soft-drink market.

1998   Cadbury Schweppes builds its first partly owned
        bottling plant with American Bottling Company.
        This appears to be the first move to consolidate
        operations. Pepsi also streamlines the company and

separates the bottling operation into the Pepsi Bottling Group.

1999   The number of bottling plants in the U.S. has fallen to 500 and the number of soft-drink companies to less than 300. U.S. population is 272,690,813.

2001   U.S. soft-drink sales grow by .5 percent, surpassing 2000 sales. Top three companies are Coke, Pepsi, and Cadbury Schweppes/ Dr Pepper/Seven Up.

2002   Cadbury Schweppes/Dr Pepper/ Seven Up has 15.6 percent market share; Coke has 43.7 percent; Pepsi has 31.6 percent. Soft-drink consumption surpasses 54 gallons per person per year.

> I . . . also grew up in Michigan (but I now live in [the] South), and I thought that it was the only ginger ale made. Needless to say, Vernor's is the only ginger ale that I will drink. My mother gave it to us kids to settle an upset stomach, and now when I go back to Michigan I make a point to have at least one cream ale (Vernor's with half & half).
> —Kim P.

2003   The growth of pay-at-the-pump gas dispensing at convenience stores has a negative effect on soft-drink sales, which show declines of 3 percent to 13 percent, depending on brand.

Mid-Continent
BOTTLER

1866-1966

OBSERVES

100TH ANNIVERSARY

Notes

1. George W. Stark, "So the Town Drinks (Free) to 70-Year-Old Beverage," *Detroit News,* July 29, 1936.

2. Ibid.

3. William T. Noble, "James Vernor's Priceless Secret," *Detroit News,* June 11, 1962.

4. Alfred W. Crosby, "Consequences of the Skirmish at Lewis Farm, March 29, 1865," *American Heritage,* 49, no. 4 (July/August 1998): 81.

5. Gyvel Young-Witzel and Michael Karl Witzel, *Soda Pop! Miracle Medicine to Pop Culture* (Stillwater, MN: Voyageur Press, 1998), 13.

6. Ibid.

7. Keith D. Wunderlich, "Deliciously Different: The Vernor's Ginger Ale Story" (manuscript, 1996).

8. Charles Herman Sulz, *Sulz's Compendium of Flavorings Containing Complete Directions for Making, Clarifying and Judiciously Applying Every Known Variety of Flavoring Extracts and Essences; Also for Preparing, Purifying and Testing Plain and Compound Syrups of Every Grade* (New York: Dick and Fitzgerald, 1888).

9. Kristine Portnoy Kelley, "Detroit's Drink," *Beverage Industry,* February 1993.

10. *Vernor's Review,* June 1966.

11. Emil A. Hiss, *The Standard Manual of Soda and Other Beverages* (Chicago: G. P. Engelhard, 1900).

12. John Fitzgibbon, "Nestor of Council: Vernor to End 25 Years' Service to Detroit," *Detroit News,* January 1, 1924.

13. "City Welfare Vernor's Aim," *Detroit News,* October 28, 1921.

14. "Councilman Vernor and His Record," *Detroit Free Press,* October 8, 1921.

15. "Vernor Hints at Counter Charge against Mayor," *Detroit Times,* February 2, 1922.

16. "Interview with Bill Henry of Stroh," *Modern Brewery Age,* January 1997.

17. Ibid.

18. Earl A. Bowkers, "The James Vernor Company," *Credit Digest,* November 1928.

19. Ibid.

20. "Judge Will Hear Vernor Co. Case," *Detroit Free Press,* December 12, 1935.

21. "Vernor's to Mark 70th Year by Giving away Ginger Ale," *Detroit News,* July 29, 1936.

22. "Detroit Has Drink on House at 70th Birthday of Vernor's," *Detroit News,* July 30, 1936.

23. Ibid.

24. Wunderlich, 6.

25. George W. Stark, "Old Timers Join Vernor's in Diamond Jubilee Toast," *Detroit News,* June 18, 1941.

26. "New Site Picked for Vernor Plant," *Detroit Free Press,* October 9, 1951.

27. George Bick, "James Vernor Company Moves to New Home," *Detroit News,* April 30, 1954.

28. Personal interview with James Vernor IV, January 20, 1999.

29. "N.Y. Group Buys Vernor's," *Detroit News,* March 28, 1966.

30. Personal interview with James Vernor IV, February 27, 1999.

31. Pete Waldemeir, "Final Toast to Another Firm," *Detroit News,* January 20, 1985.

32. Peter Garilovich, "Vernor's Plans to Leave City," *Detroit Free Press,* January 20, 1985.

33. Joseph Menn, "Vernor's Chances of Staying Home Look Up," *Detroit Free Press,* June 24, 1986.

34. Joy Bennett Josey, "Vernor's Plant to Tumble for Shopping Mall," *Crain's Detroit Business,* November 9–15, 1987.

35. Doug Sword, "AFC Gains 8 Percent Interest in A&W through Vernor's Sale," *Cincinnati Business,* December 1987.

36. John Jordan, "After the Crash: A&W Success Rooted in Niche Markets," *Westchester County Business Journal,* April 1988, 47.

37. Jennifer Lawrence and Patricia Strand, "A&W Spices up Lineup: Will New Owner Move It National?" *Advertising Age,* August 31, 1987, 27.

38. Ibid.

39. Personal interview with Ron Bialecki, October 1998.

40. Rick Ratliff, "Acquired a Taste for Corvettes? Tell It to Vernor's," *Detroit Free Press,* April 17, 1989.

Bibliography

Asbury, Herbert. *The Great Illusion: An Informal History of Prohibition.* New York: Greenwood, 1968.

Babson, Steve. *Building the Union: Skilled Workers and Anglo-Gaelic Immigrants in the Rise of the UAW.* New Brunswick, NJ: Rutgers University Press, 1991.

———. *Working Detroit: The Making of a Union Town.* New York: Adama Books, 1984.

Bak, Richard. *Cobb Would Have Caught It: The Golden Age of Baseball in Detroit.* Detroit: Wayne State University Press, 1991.

Banfield, Edward C. *Big-City Politics: A Comparative Guide to the Political Systems of Atlanta, Boston, Detroit, El Paso, Los Angeles, Miami, Philadelphia, St. Louis [and] Seattle.* New York: Random House, 1965.

Beasley, Norman, and George W. Stark. *Made in Detroit.* New York: Putnam, 1957.

Bingay, Malcolm Wallace. *Detroit Is My Hometown.* New York: Bobbs-Merrill, 1946.

Burton, C. M. *Early Detroit: A Sketch of Some of the Interesting Affairs of the Olden Time.* [Detroit], 1909.

Capeci, Dominic. *Layered Violence: The Detroit Rioters of 1943.* Jackson: University Press of Mississippi, 1991.

Chardoul, Paul N. "The Fourth Michigan Cavalry: A Civil War Regimental History." Master's thesis, East Lansing, Michigan State University, Department of History, 1964.

Coffey, Thomas M. *The Long Thirst: Prohibition in America 1920–1933.* New York: Norton, 1975.

Committee of Merchants for the Relief of Colored People Suffering from the Late Riots. *Anti-Negro Riots in the North, 1863.* New York: Arno Press, 1863.

Conference Board. *The Detroit Market, 1972/1973: Based on a Survey Conducted by the United States Bureau of the Census.* New York: Conference Board, 1975.

Conot, Robert E. *American Odyssey.* New York: Morrow, 1974.

Curtis, O. B. *History of the Twenty-fourth Michigan of the Iron Brigade: Known as the Detroit and Wayne County Regiment.* Gaithersburg, MD: Olde Soldier Books, 1988.

Darden, Joe T., et al. *Detroit, Race, and Uneven Development.* Philadelphia: Temple University Press, 1987.

Davis, Donald Finlay. *Conspicuous Production: Automobiles and Cities in Detroit, 1899–1933.* Philadelphia: Temple University Press, 1988.

Ewen, Lynda Ann. *Corporate Power and Urban Crisis in Detroit.* Princeton: Princeton University Press, 1978.

Ferman, Louis A. *Death of a Newspaper: The Story of the Detroit Times: A Study of Job Dislocation among Newspaper Workers in a Depressed Labor Market.* Kalamazoo, MI: W. E. Upjohn Institute for Employment Research, 1963.

Ferry, W. Hawkins. *The Buildings of Detroit: A History.* Detroit: Wayne State University Press, 1968.

First National Bank of Detroit. *Highlights of Detroit History in Miniature: A Series of Models First Displayed at the Opening of the Fisher Building Branch, October 22, 1928.* Detroit: First National Bank of Detroit, [1929?].

Haines, David H., and United States Army. "Michigan Cavalry Regiment, 4th (1862–1865)." Manuscript, 1865.

Henrickson, Wilma Wood, ed. *Detroit Perspectives: Crossroads and Turning Points.* Detroit: Wayne State University Press, 1991.

Herron, Jerry. *AfterCulture: Detroit and the Humiliation of History.* Detroit: Wayne State University Press, 1993.

Hiss, Emil A. *The Standard Manual of Soda and Other Beverages.* Chicago: G. P. Engelhard, 1900.

Hyde, Charles K. *Detroit: An Industrial History Guide.* Detroit: Detroit Historical Society, [1980?].

Jeffries, Edward. *Detroit and the "Good War": The World War II Letters of Mayor Edward Jeffries and Friends.* Lexington: University Press of Kentucky, 1966.

Jones, D. D., and J. William. *The Davis Memorial Volume or our Dead President: Jefferson Davis and the World's Tribute to His Memory.* Richmond, VA: B. F. Johnson, 1890.

Kobler, John. *Ardent Spirits: The Rise and Fall of Prohibition.* New York: Putnam, 1973.

Lakey, Roland T. "James Vernor: 1843–1897." Unpublished speech, Kremer's Reference Files, University of Wisconsin, Madison, Health Sciences, date unknown.

Laut, Agnes C. *Cadillac: Knight Errant of the Wilderness, Founder of Detroit, Governor of Louisiana from the Great Lakes to the Gulf.* Indianapolis: Bobbs-Merrill, 1931.

Leggett, John C. *Class, Race, and Labor: Working-Class Consciousness in Detroit.* New York: Oxford University Press, 1968.

Lichtenstein, Nelson. *Walter Reuther: The Most Dangerous Man in Detroit.* Urbana: University of Illinois Press, [1997?].

Lincoln, James H. *The Anatomy of Riot: A Judge's Report.* New York: McGraw-Hill, 1968.

Lochbiler, Don. *Detroit's Coming of Age, 1873 to 1973.* Detroit: Wayne State University Press, 1973.

Lutz, William W. *The News of Detroit: How a Newspaper and City Grew Together.* Boston: Little, Brown, 1973.

Mason, Philip. *The Ambassador Bridge: A Monument to Progress.* Detroit: Wayne State University Press, 1987.

Meier, August, and Elliott Rudwick. *Black Detroit and the Rise of the UAW.* New York: Oxford University Press, 1979.

Merz, Charles. *The Dry Decade.* Seattle: University of Washington Press, 1969.

Miral, Jeffrey. *The Rise and Fall of an Urban School System: Detroit, 1907–81.* Ann Arbor: University of Michigan Press, 1993.

Moon, Elaine Latzman. *Untold Tales, Unsung Heroes: An Oral History of Detroit's African-American Community, 1918–1967.* Detroit: Wayne State University Press, 1994.

National Soft Drink Association. Internet site, <www.nsda.org>, 1998.

O'Geran, Graeme. *A History of the Detroit Street Railways.* Detroit: Conover Press, 1931.

Parkins, A. E. *The Historical Geography of Detroit.* Lansing: Michigan Historical Commission, 1918.

Pound, Arthur. *Detroit: Dynamic City.* New York: Appleton-Century, 1940.

Quaife, M. M. *This Is Detroit: Two Hundred and Fifty Years in Pictures.* Detroit: Wayne State University Press, 1951.

Rich, Wilbur C. *Black Mayors and School Politics: The Failure of Reform in Detroit, Gary, and Newark.* New York: Garland Publishing, 1996.

Schneider, John C. *Detroit and the Problem of Order, 1830–1880: A Geography of Crime, Riot, and Policing.* Lincoln: University of Nebraska Press, 1980.

Sulz, Charles Herman. *Sulz's Compendium of Flavorings Containing Complete Directions for Making, Clarifying and Judiciously Applying Every Known Variety of Flowering Extracts and Essences; Also for Preparing, Purifying and Testing Plain and Compound Syrups of Every Grade.* New York: Dick and Fitzgerald, 1888.

University of Michigan, Urban Design Studio. *Cass Corridor: Profile and Policies.* Ann Arbor: The Studio, 1976.

U.S. Census. Per Capita Consumption of Selected Beverages, by Type: 1980 to 1996. Table 249 *in Statistical Abstract of the United States,* 118th ed., 157. Washington, DC: U.S. Government Printing Office, 1998.

Widick, B. J. *Detroit: City of Race and Class Violence.* Detroit: Wayne State University Press, 1989.

Woodbury, Frank Bury. *All Our Yesterdays: A Brief History of Detroit.* Detroit: Wayne State University Press, 1969.

Wunderlich, Keith D. "Deliciously Different: The Vernor's Ginger Ale Story." Manuscript, 1996.

Young-Witzel, Gyvel, and Michael Karl Witzel. *Soda Pop! Miracle Medicine to Pop Culture.* Stillwater, MN: Voyageur Press, 1998.

Acknowledgments

The author is grateful to Ron Bialecki for many of the images used in this volume.

I want to offer special thanks to Ron "the Gnome" Bialecki and Jim Knott, whose idea it was to write this book in the first place. Ron supplied a major portion of the photographs and illustrations and has been an inspiration in writing this book. Ron, of course, is the real, live Vernor's gnome, who expended many hours following up on leads and contacting people in spite of his failing health. Jim has done a lot of the endless legwork in tracking down various resources and people. In addition, James Vernor IV and his wife, Jackie, provided information that could not have been obtained in any other way, and for this I am grateful.

In this age of electronic publishing it is a great comfort to have talented people that you can depend on to help you create files and overcome problems involved in the creation of illustrations on the computer. This task fell into the capable hands of Gary Guerriero of Sundyne Corporation, who spent many hours of his own time at home creating, scanning, and cleaning the artwork. Additional help in this regard came from Michelle Waddell and Mark Squire, who both helped in the restoration and scanning of the older photographs. I send special thanks to artist Bill Moss and his agent, Martha Polacsek, of Captain of the Fleet, Inc., for the use of his beautiful Detroit riverfront painting titled *Detroit's Traditions,* which appears herein.

A historical account such as this also requires a great deal of research, and much of this task fell on David L. Poremba of the Detroit Public Library Burton Historical Collection. David spent many hours researching the Vernor family and helping me locate information. Professor Doug Ernest of Colorado State University must be thanked for helping proof the historical facts and correcting content errors. Additional recognition and thanks are offered to Tom Moothart, a librarian at Colorado State University, for assisting with my frequent requests for help.

Chricinda McGee got her research feet wet at the beginning of the project and helped to get me started through the long process of discovery. Jack Deo of Superior View/Michigan View in Marquette, Michigan, supplied additional information and photos.

I also thank W. B. Doner, Mort Feigenson of the Faygo Company, Eilene Hamel of the Spirit of Detroit Association, Robert Greer, Hyatt and Millie Eby, John and Martha Polacsek, Jean Bialecki, Kevin and Beth Bialecki, Bill Buechel, Leroy Goodall, Robert Cannon, and Kim Denton and Kelli Freeman of the Dr Pepper/Seven Up, Inc., Division of Cadbury Schweppes. Last, but not least, special thanks to Mary Erwin and Kelly Sippell of the University of Michigan Press for their hard work in seeing this project through to completion.

Without the generous help of all these people I would not have been able to complete this task.